WELCOME TO
THE BIG BOOK OF 100 ANTIQUE BOTANICAL DESIGNS TO COLOR
-AN ADULT COLORING BOOK -

100 ANTIQUE DESIGNS ON SINGLE-SIDED PAGES

THE DESIGNS IN THIS BOOK ARE ADAPTED FROM ORIGINAL 18TH AND 19TH CENTURY BOTANICAL ART. WE HAVE PAINSTAKINGLY DIGITALLY REMOVED THE WATER SPOTS, FOXING AND OTHER DAMAGE FROM THE ORIGINAL IMAGES IN ORDER TO CONVERT THEM TO BLACK AND WHITE DRAWINGS FOR YOU TO COLOR.

COPYRIGHTS ON ALL THE ORIGINALS HAVE LONG EXPIRED BUT, IN FACT, WE THINK THE ORIGINAL ARTISTS WOULD BE HONORED AND EXCITED TO KNOW THERE ARE STILL MANY OF US WHO CONTINUE TO APPRECIATE THEIR WORK BY CREATING OUR OWN VERSIONS OF THEIR WORKS CELEBRATING MOTHER NATURE.

SOME DESIGNS IN THIS BOOK ARE RELATIVELY EASY TO COMPLETE WHILE YOU MAY FIND OTHER DESIGNS A BIT MORE INTRICATE AND CHALLENGING. THERE IS NO RIGHT OR WRONG COLOR OR DESIGN SO BE AS CREATIVE OR TRADITIONAL AS YOU WISH.

THE MOST IMPORTANT PART IS TO RELAX AND HAVE FUN!

WHEN COMPLETED, THESE 8 X 10 IMAGES WILL FIT PERFECTLY INTO THE STANDARD OPENING OF AN 11 X 14 MAT FOR FRAMING.

FOR INFORMATION ON ALL OUR BOOKS PLEASE VISIT OUR WEBSITE AT WWW.BOTANICALARTDESIGNS.COM

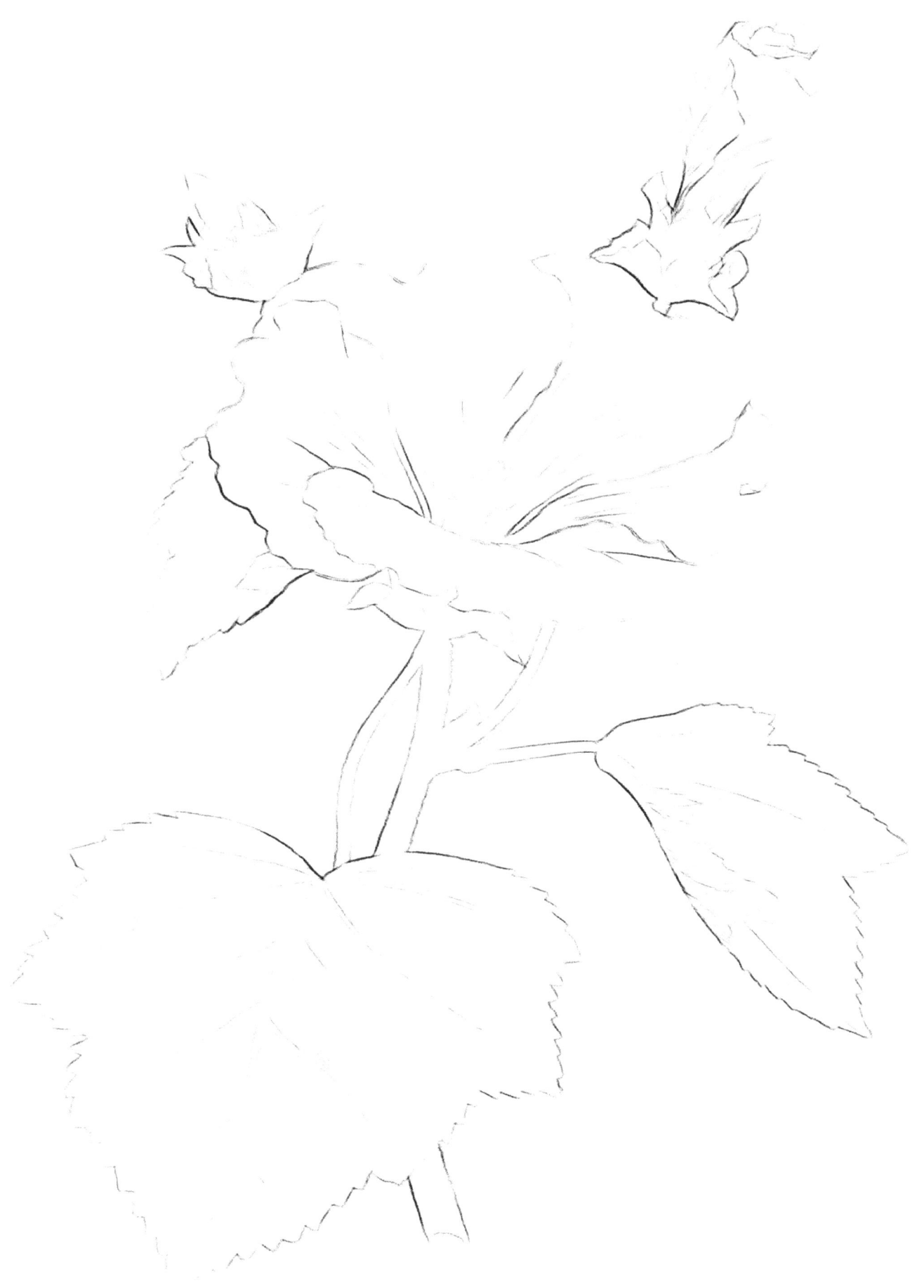

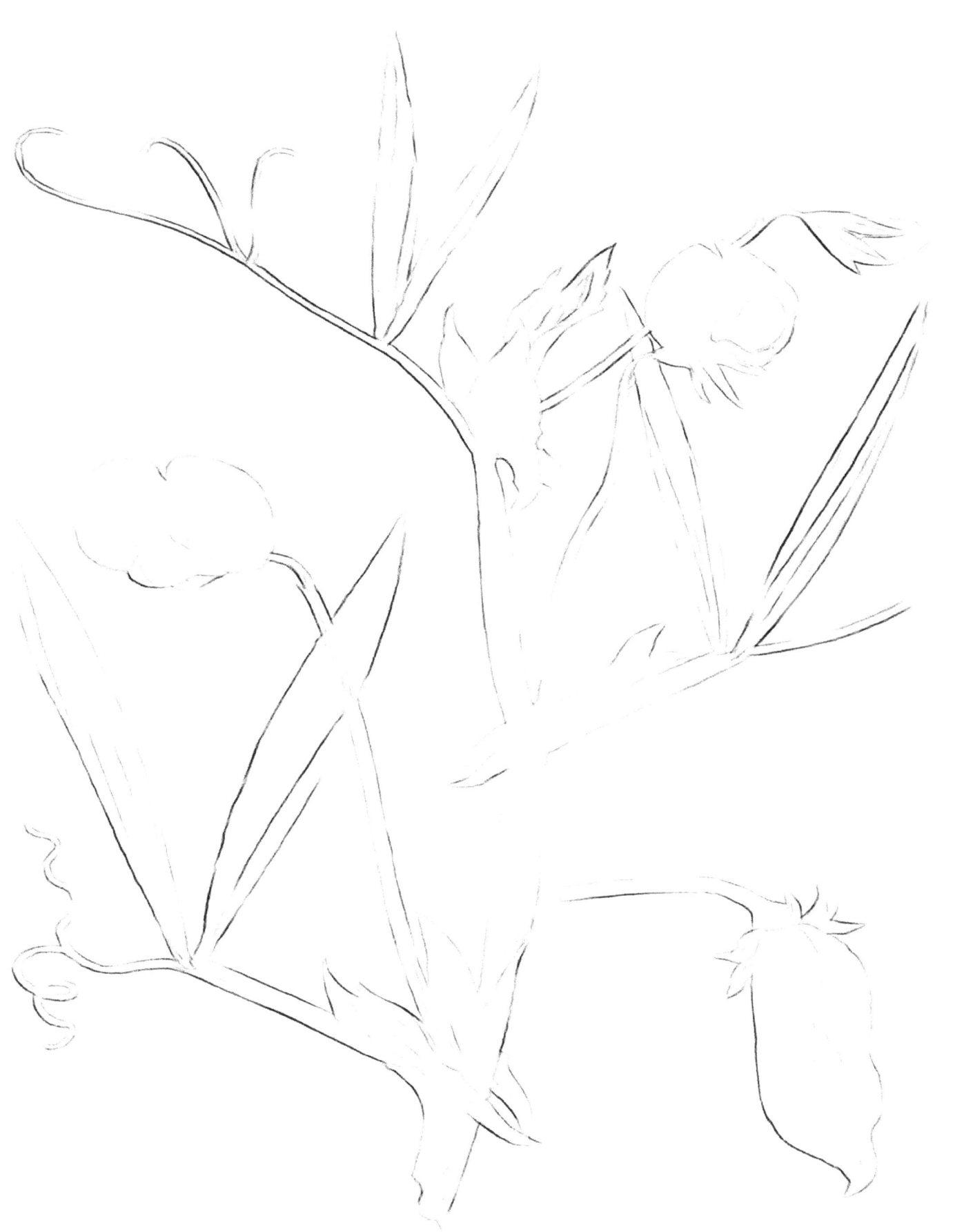

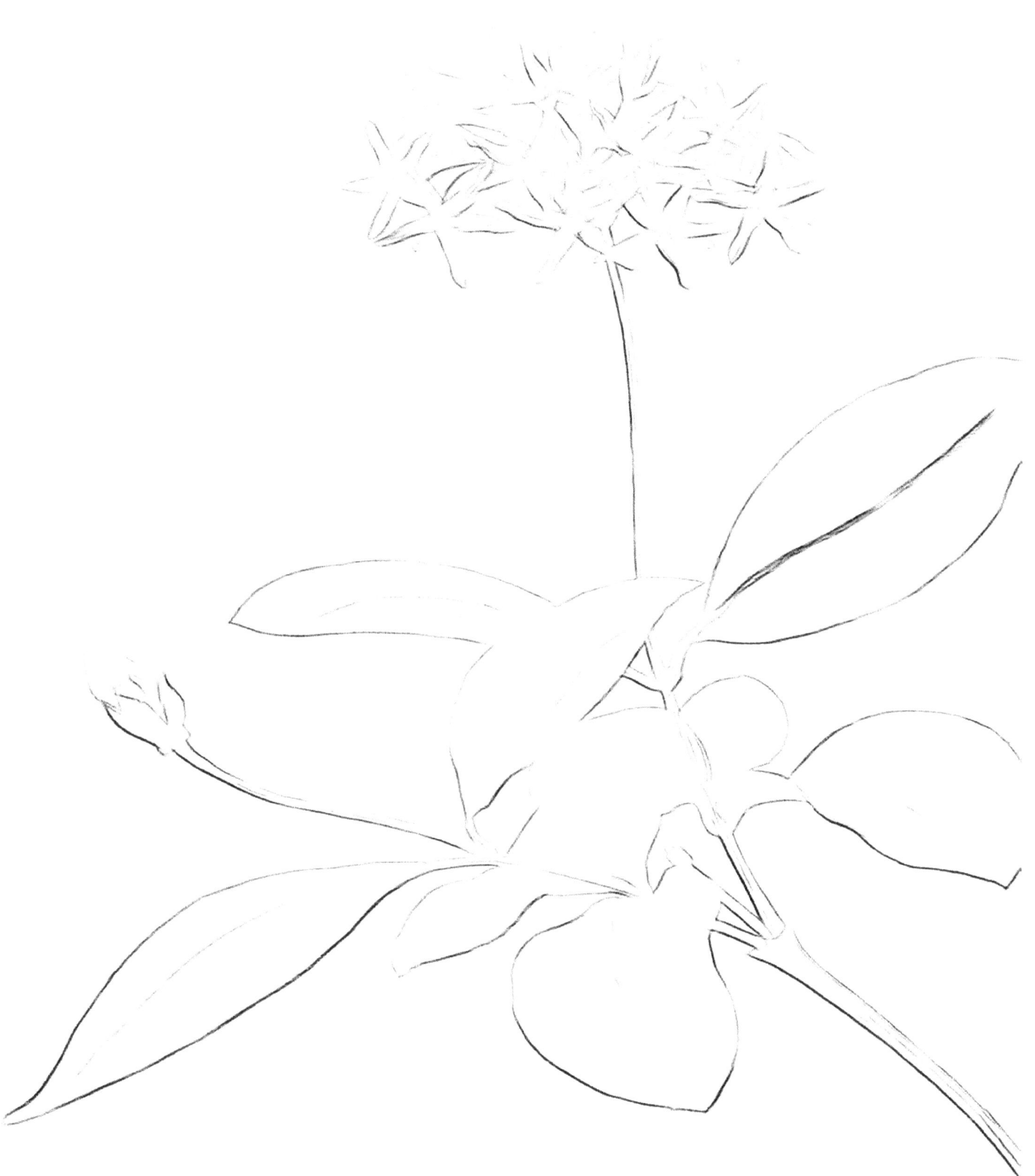

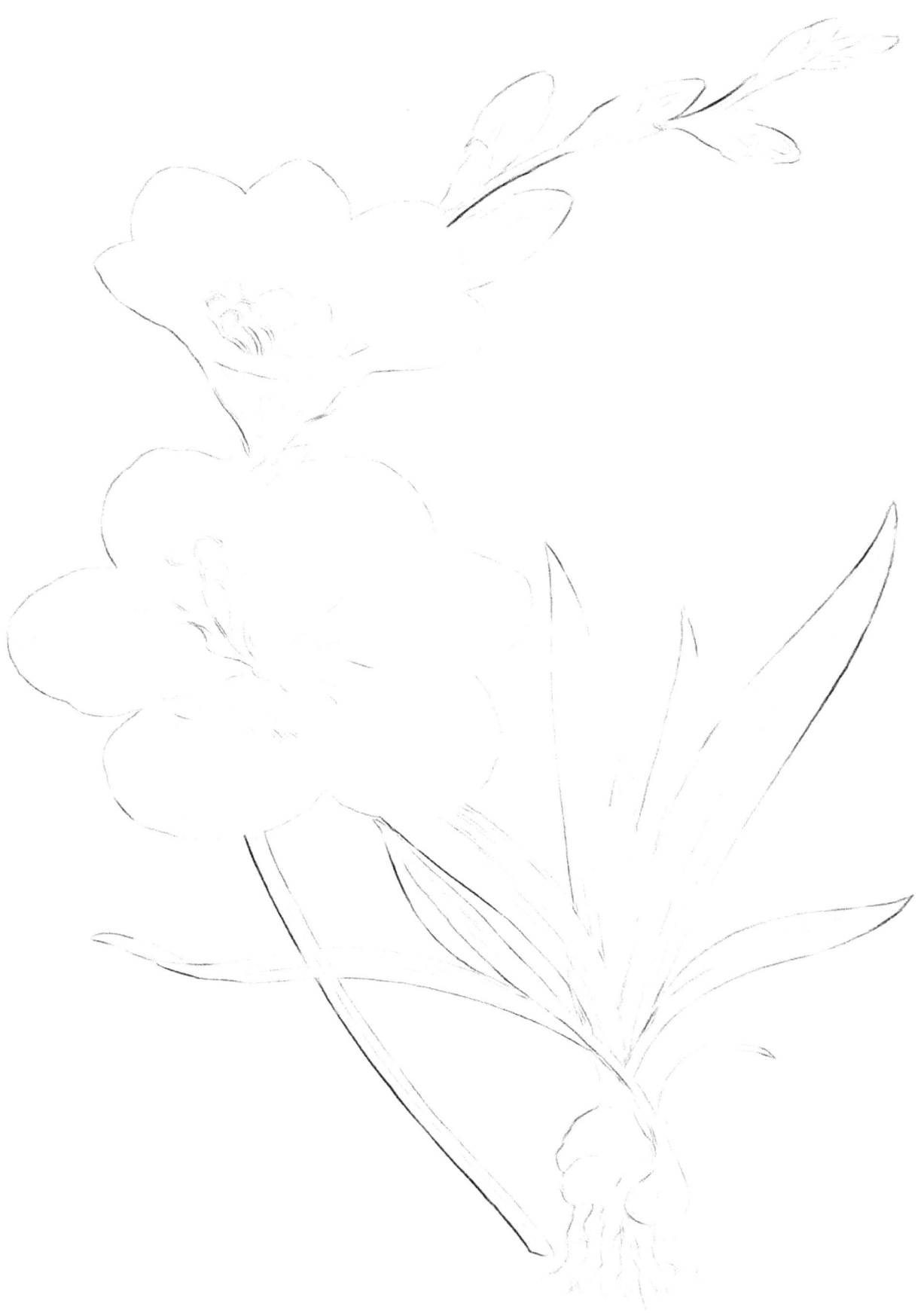

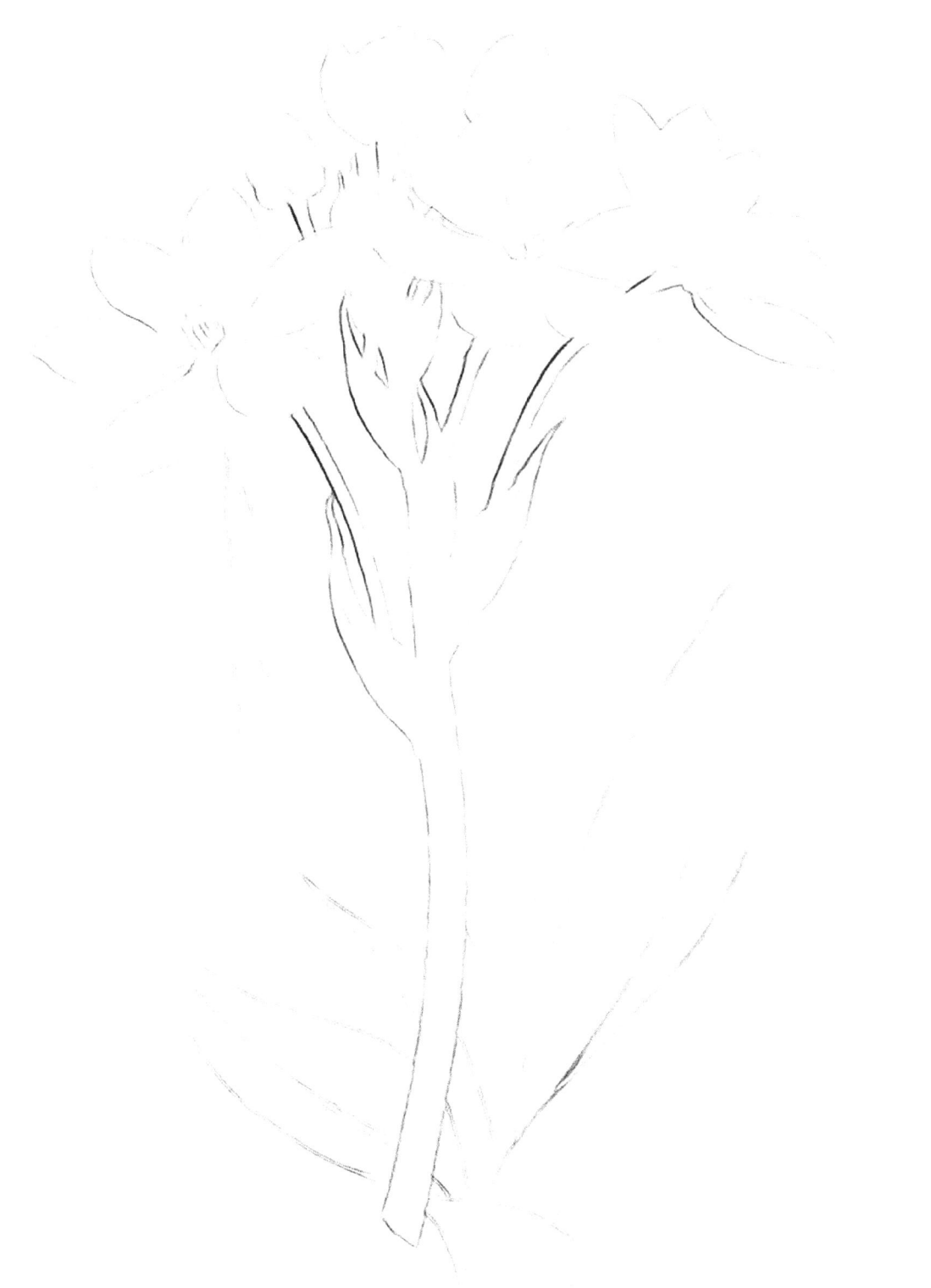

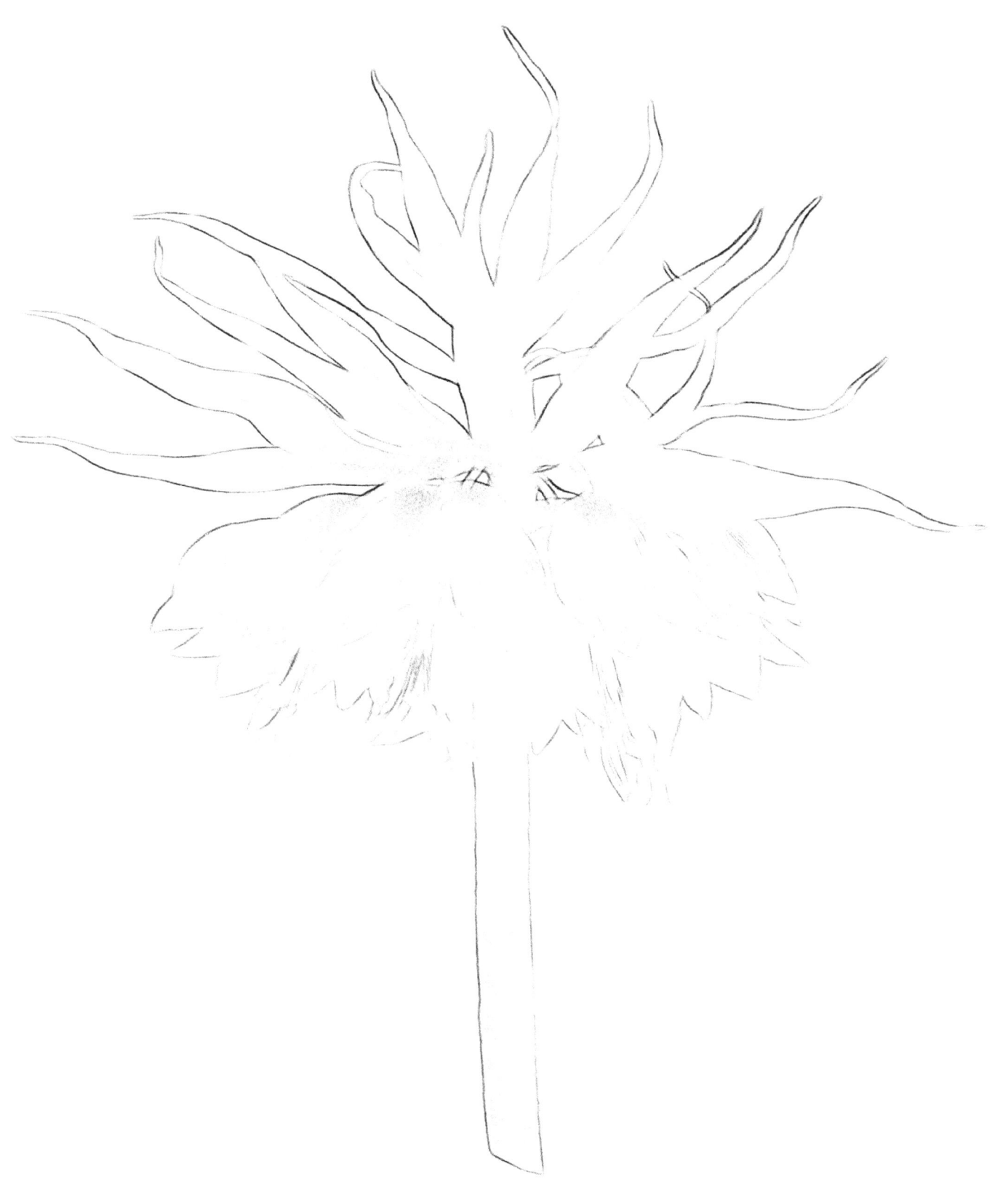

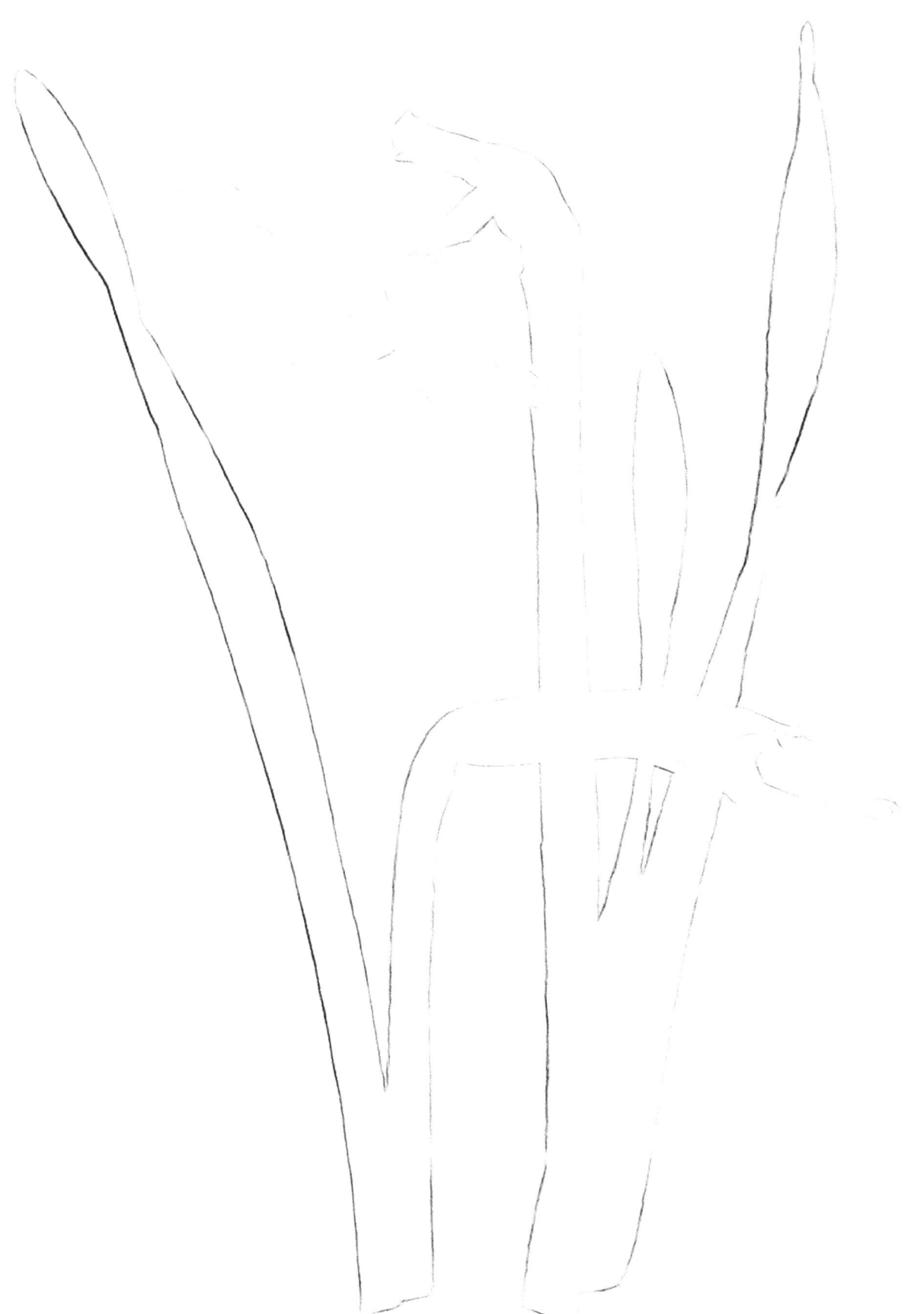

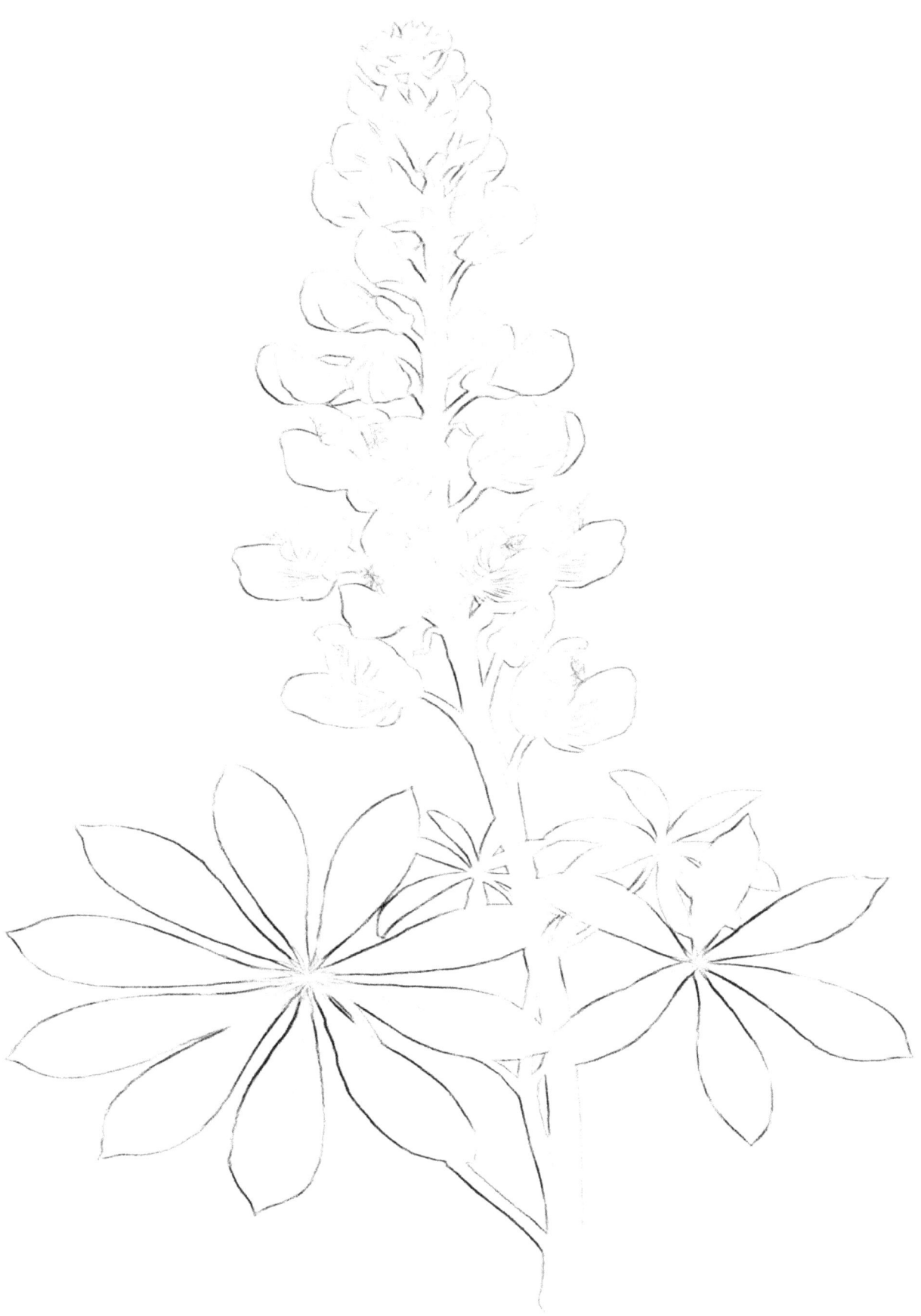

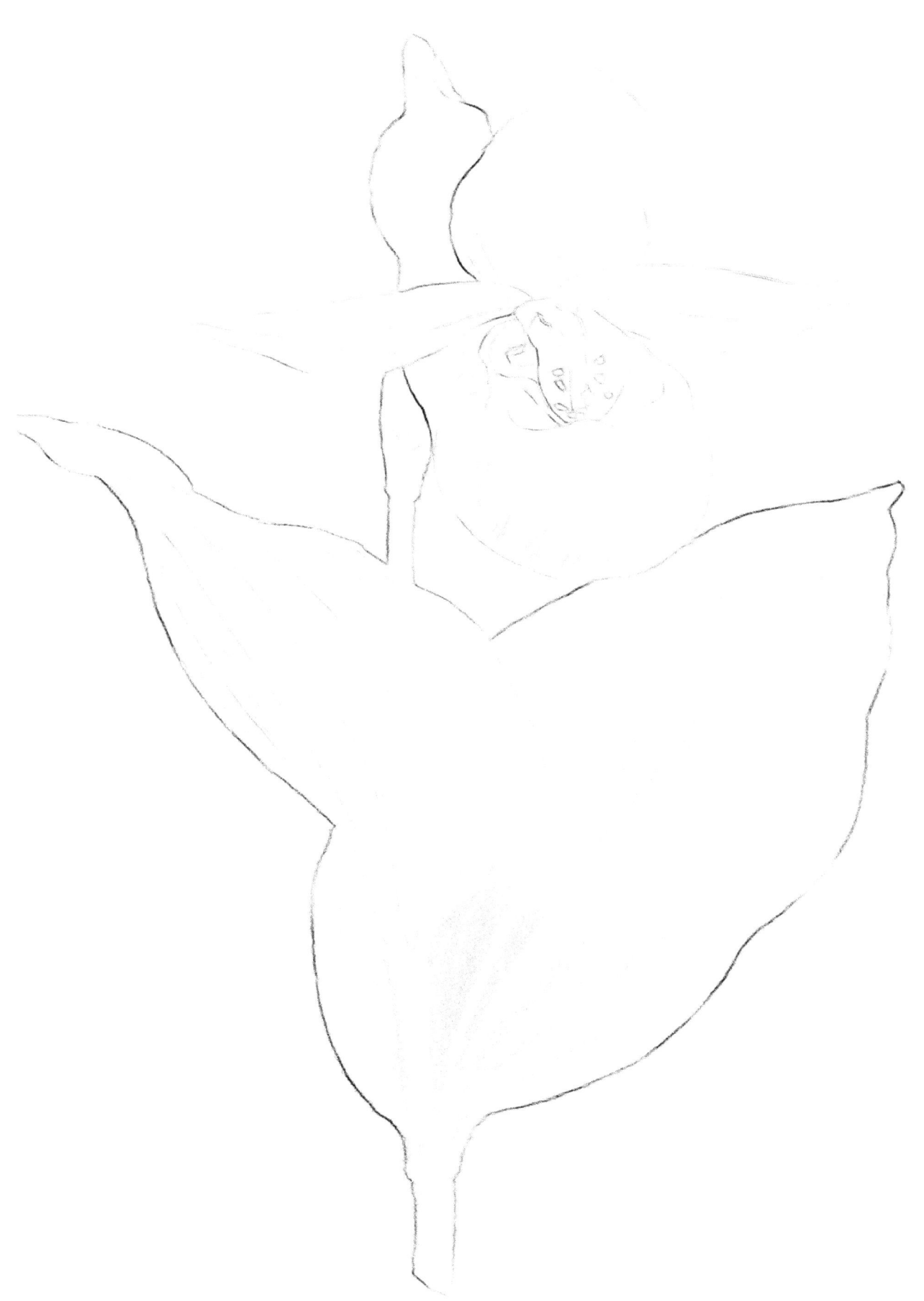

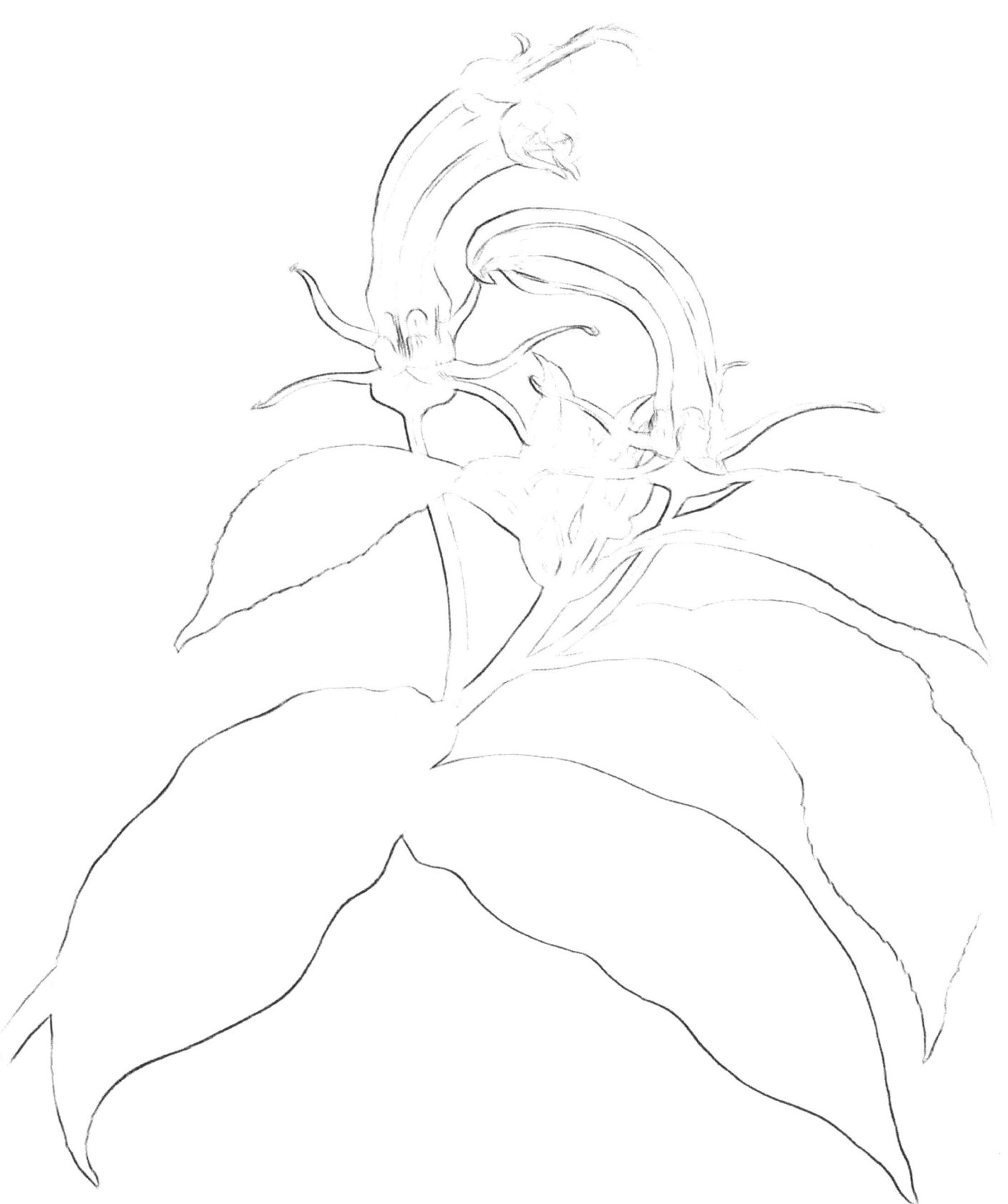

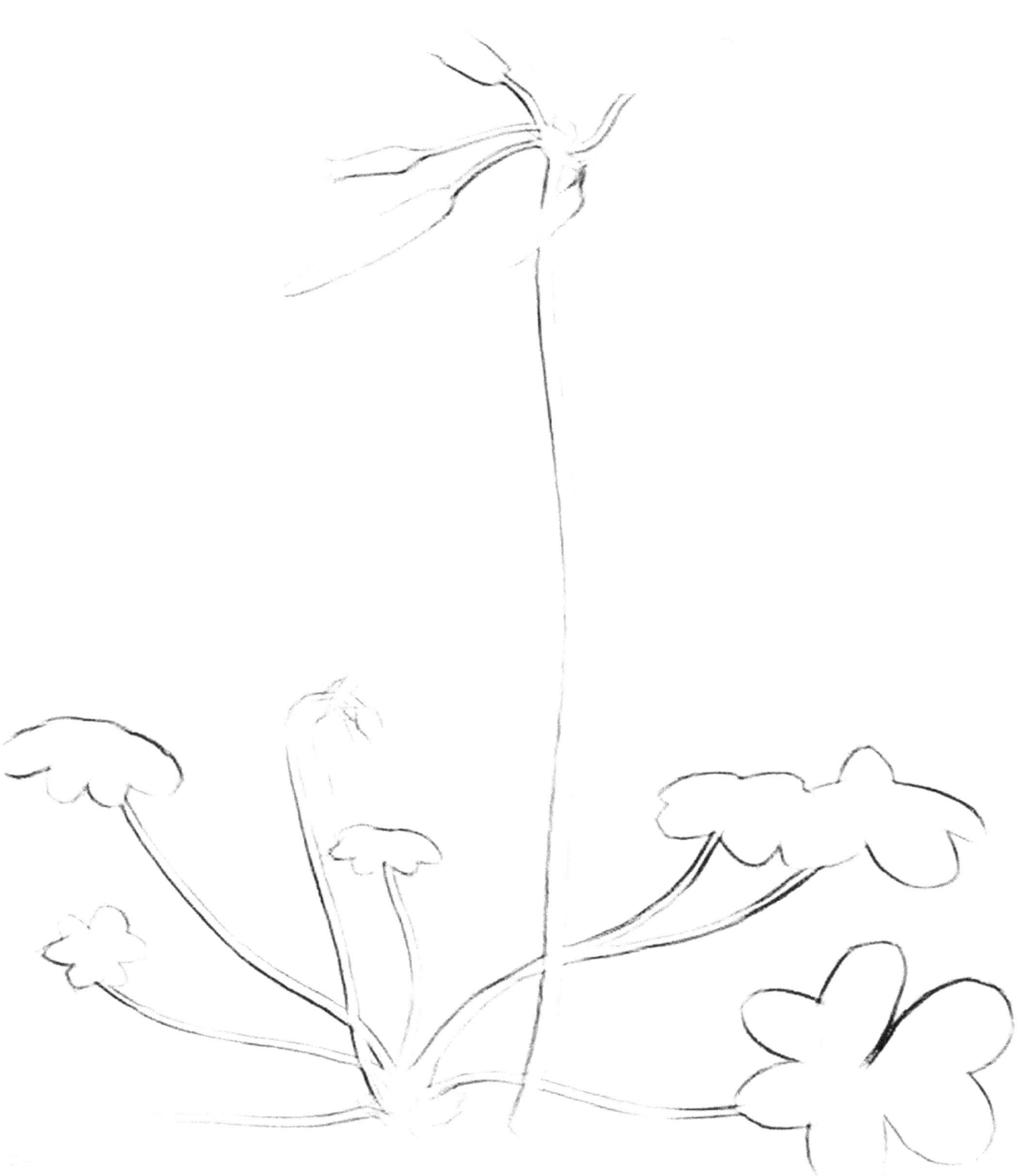

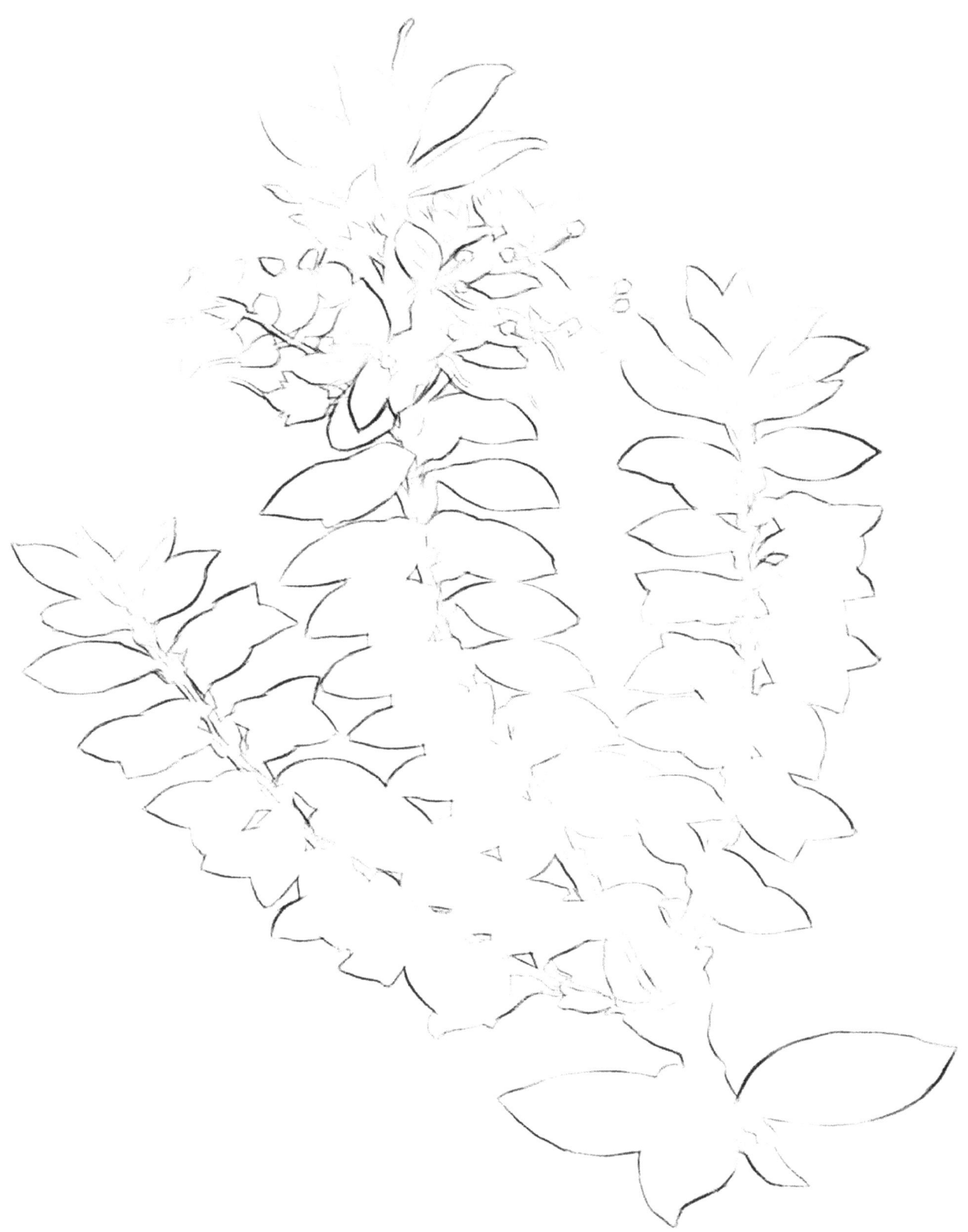

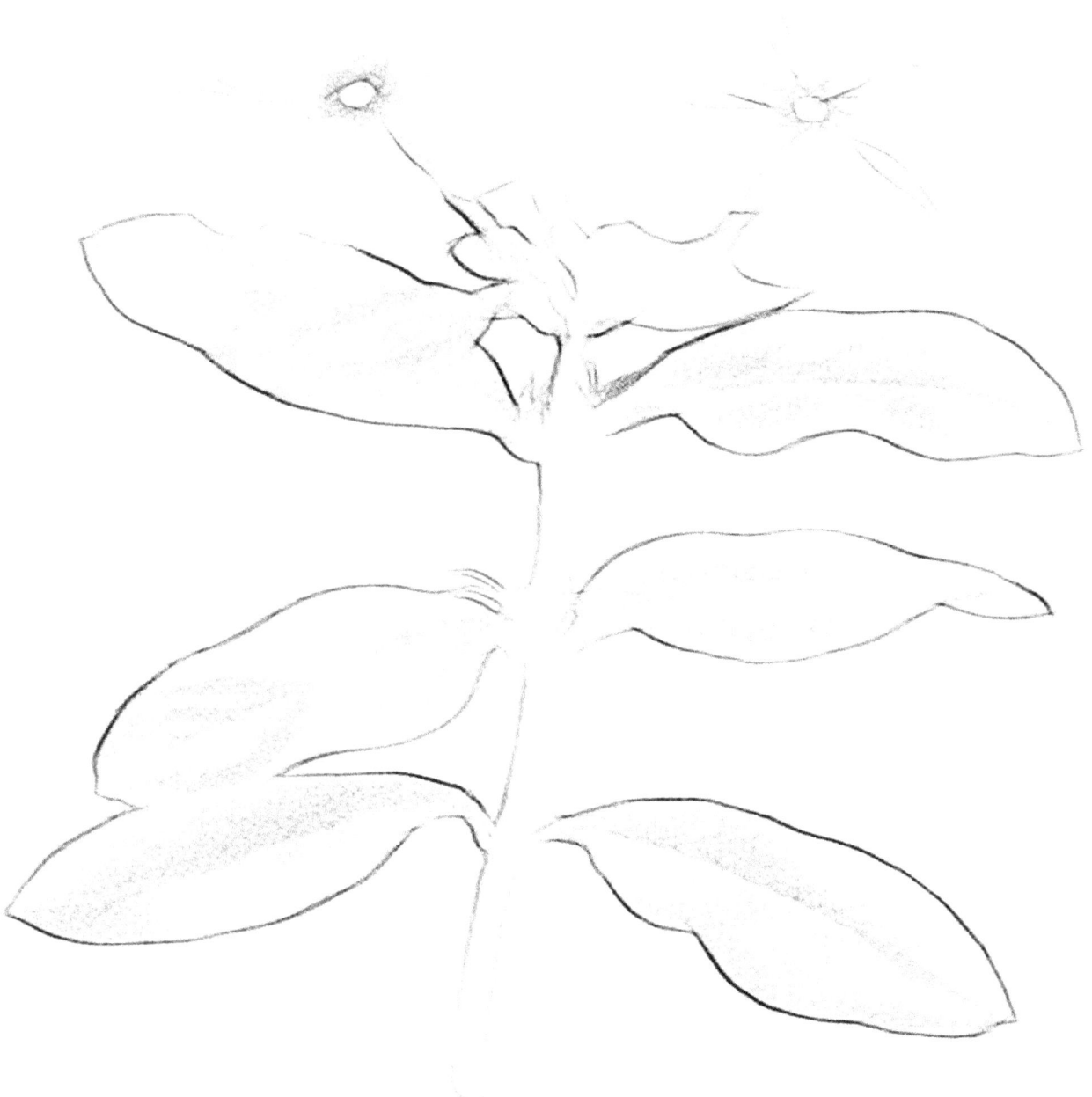

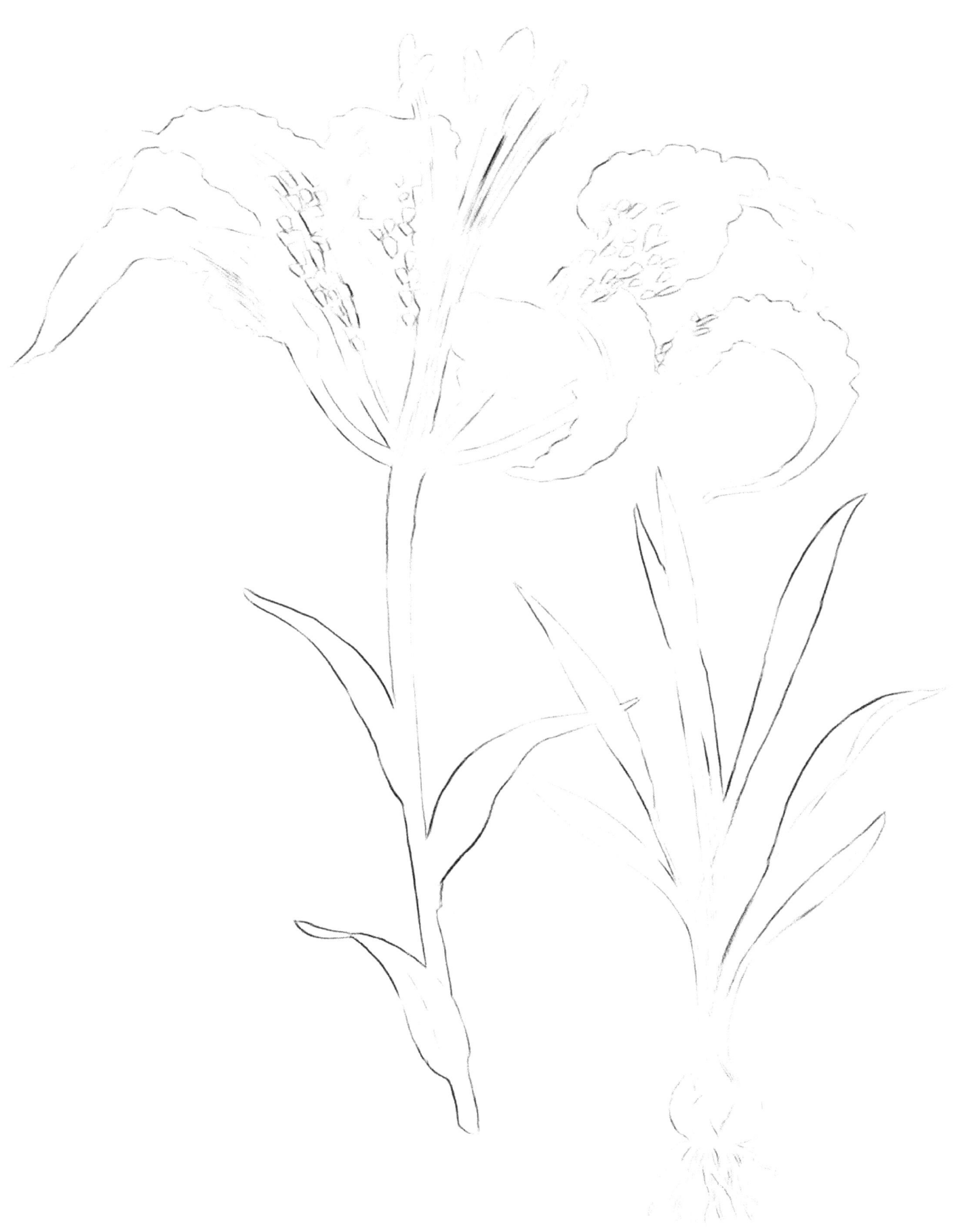

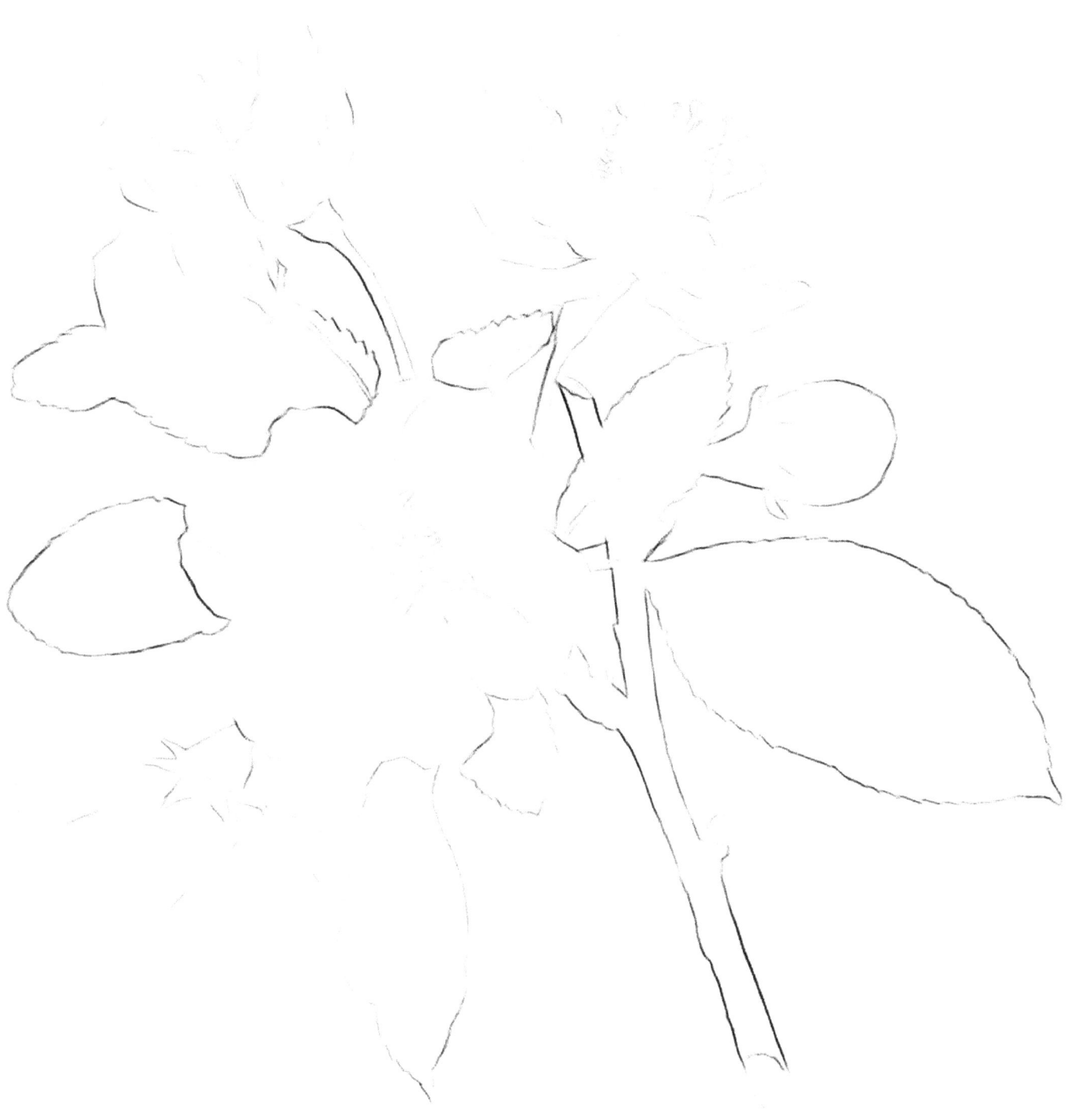

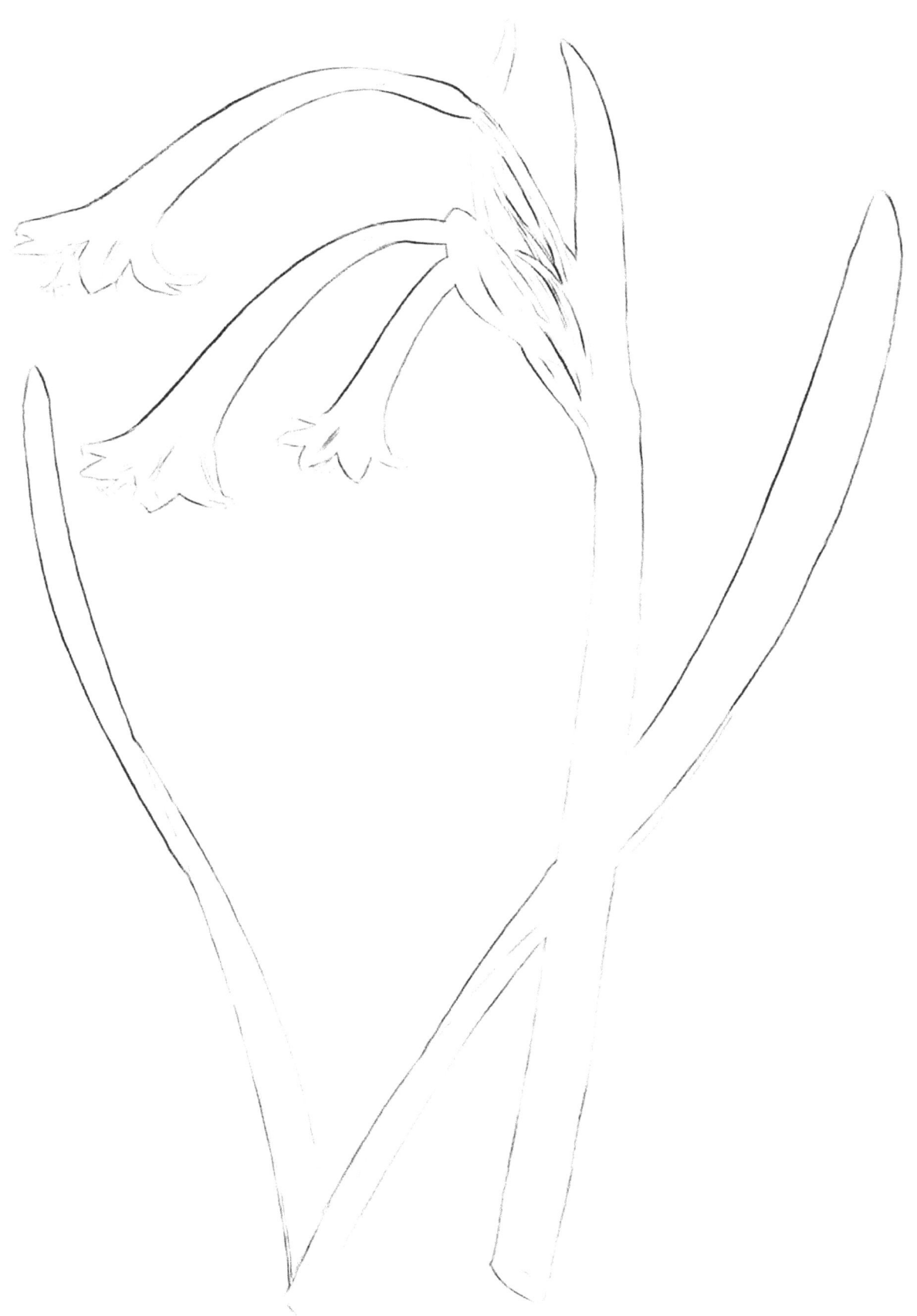

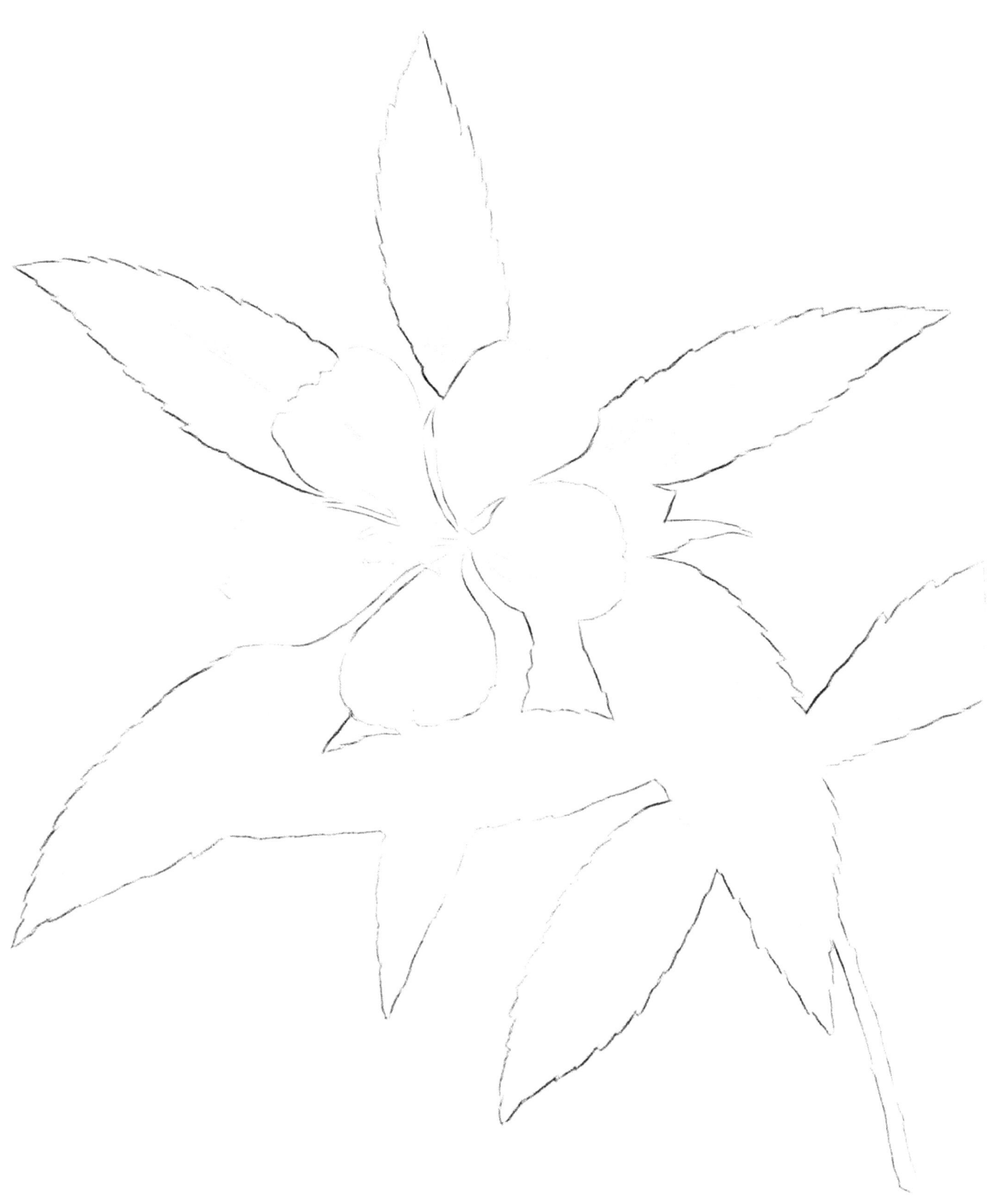

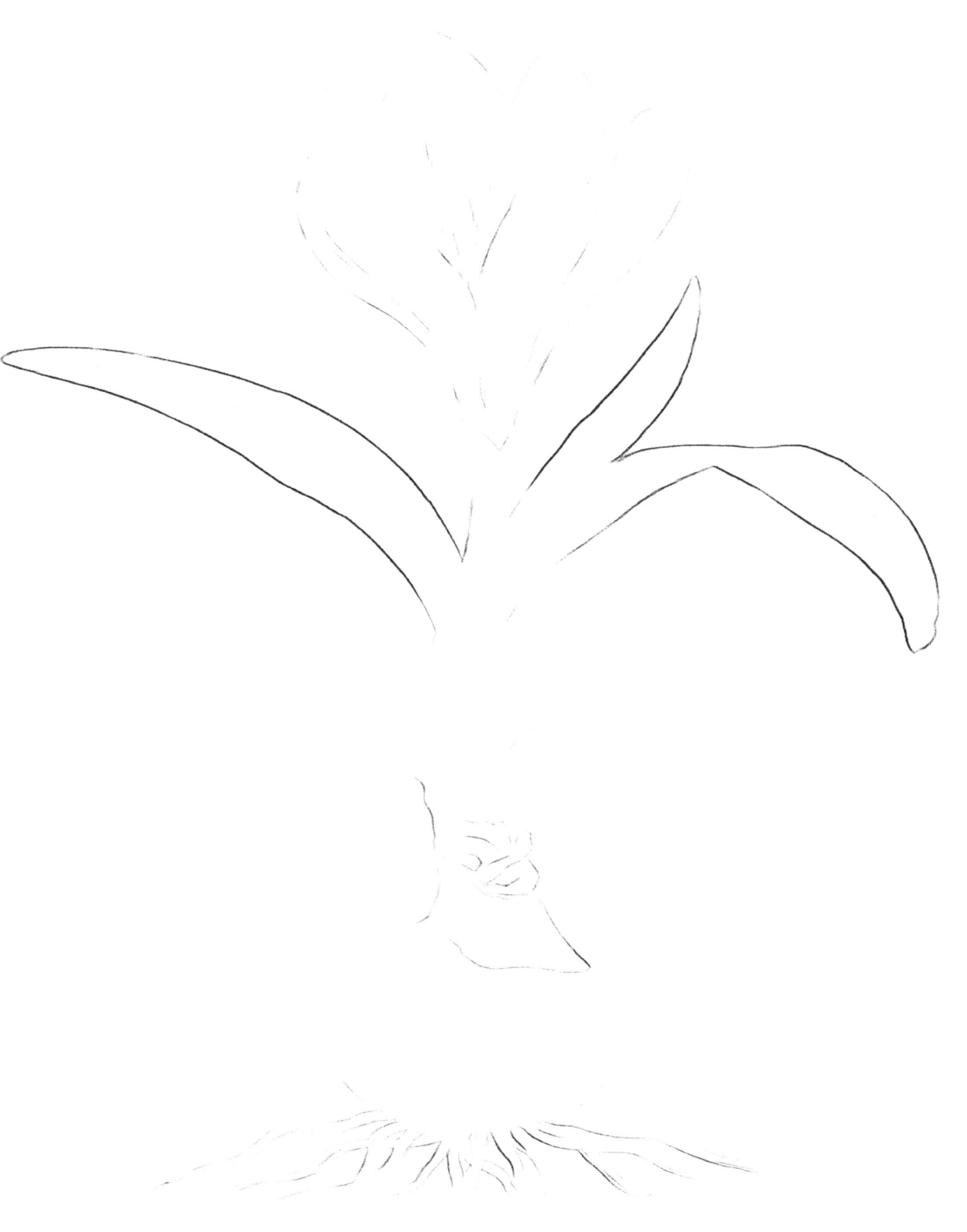

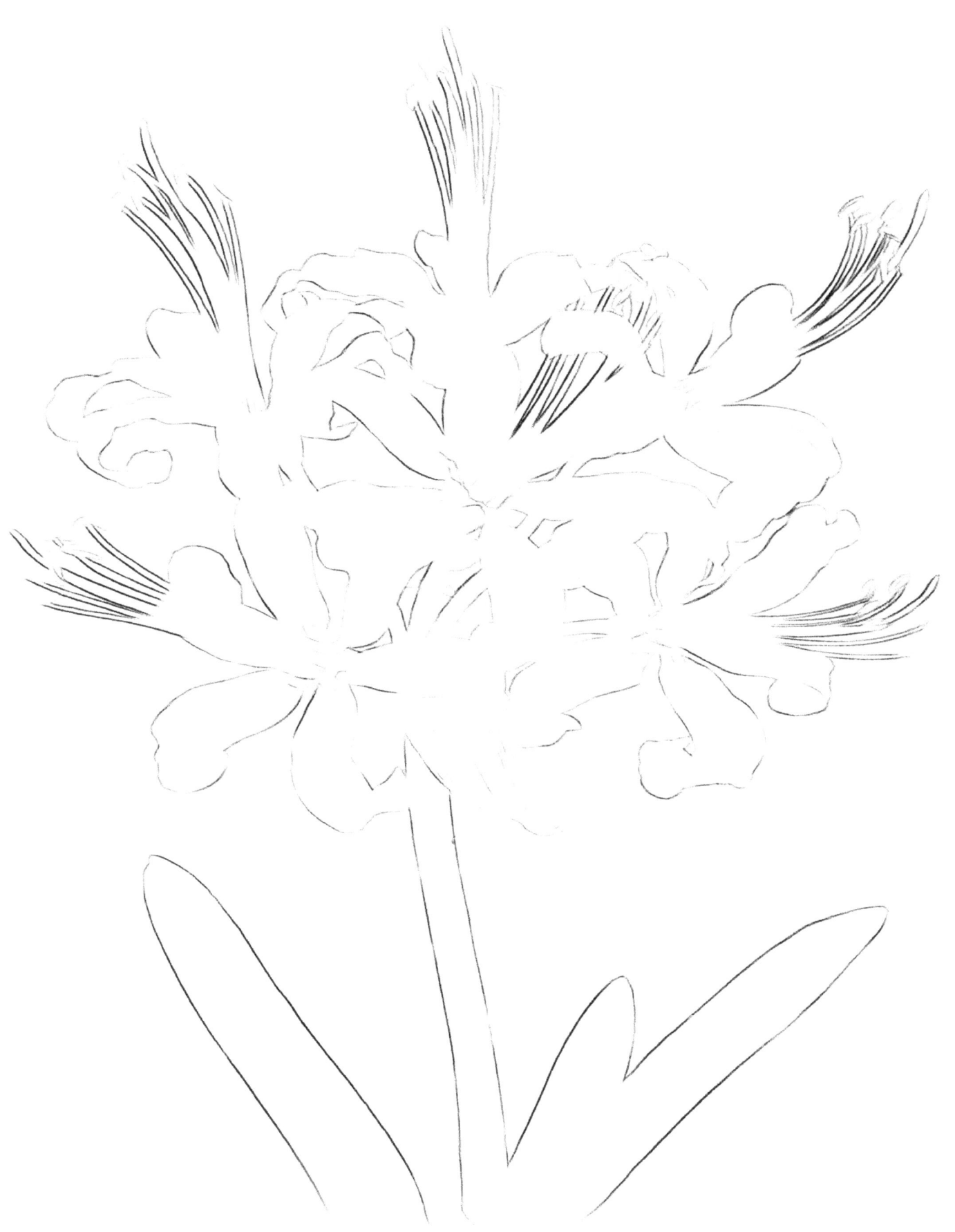

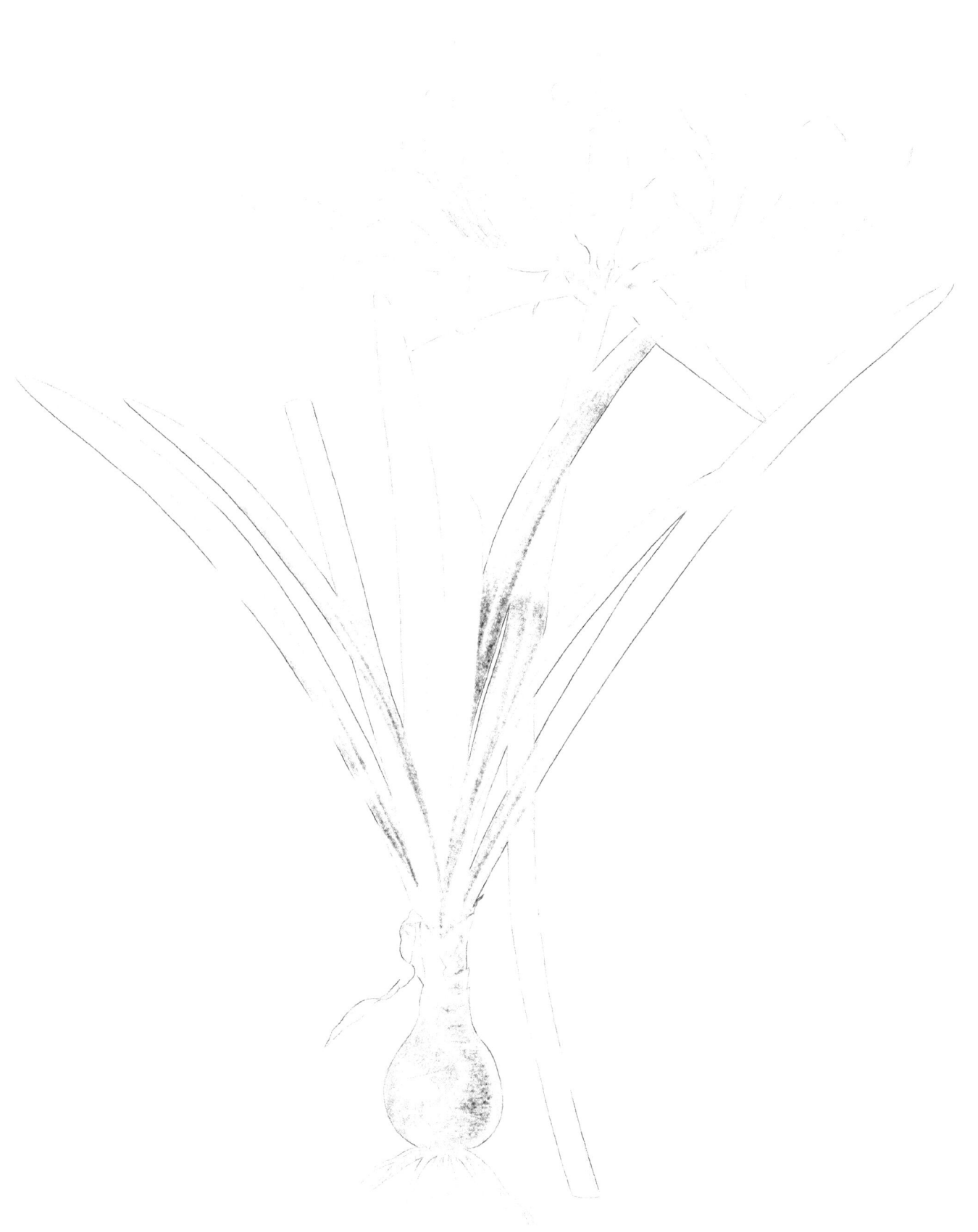

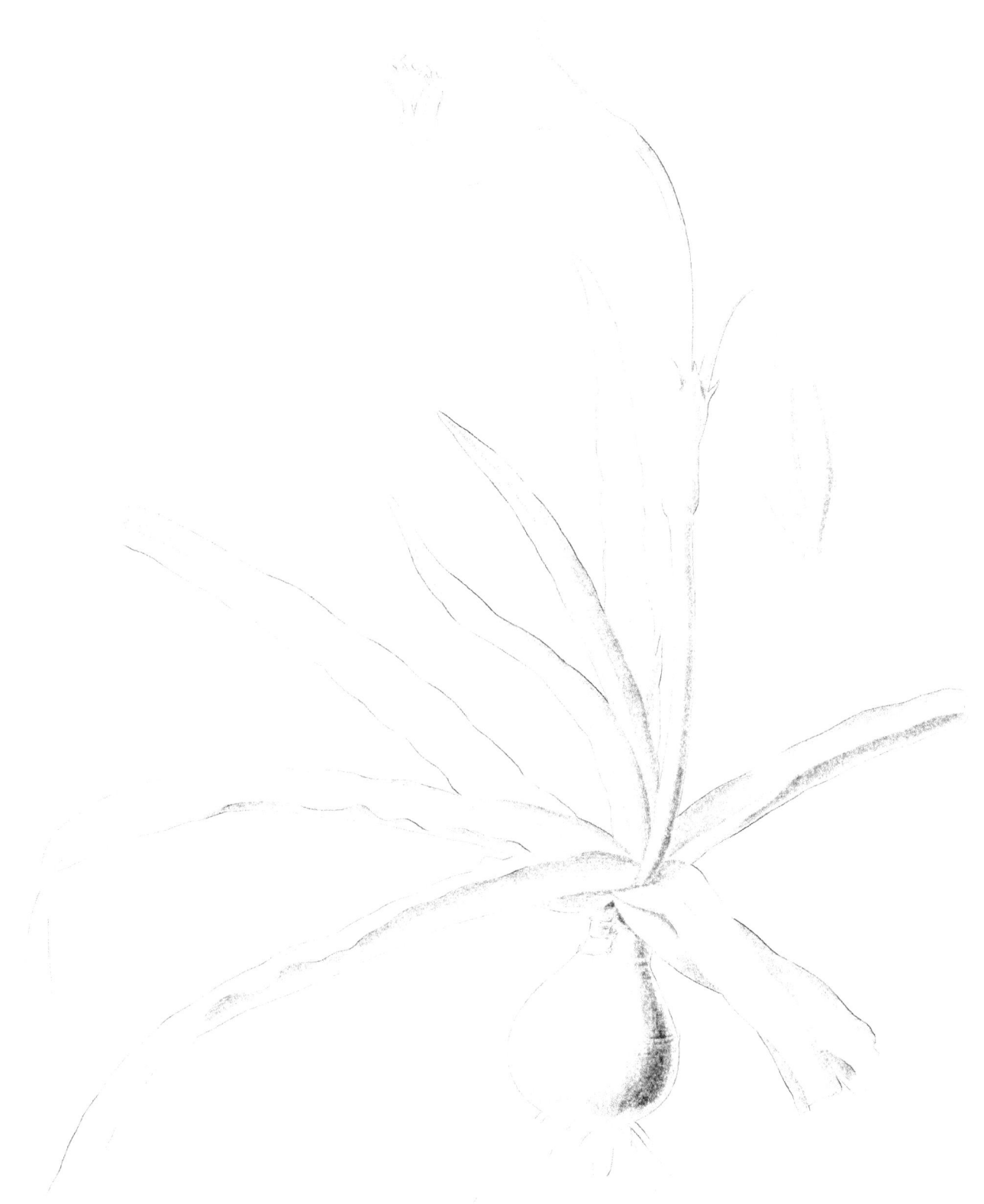

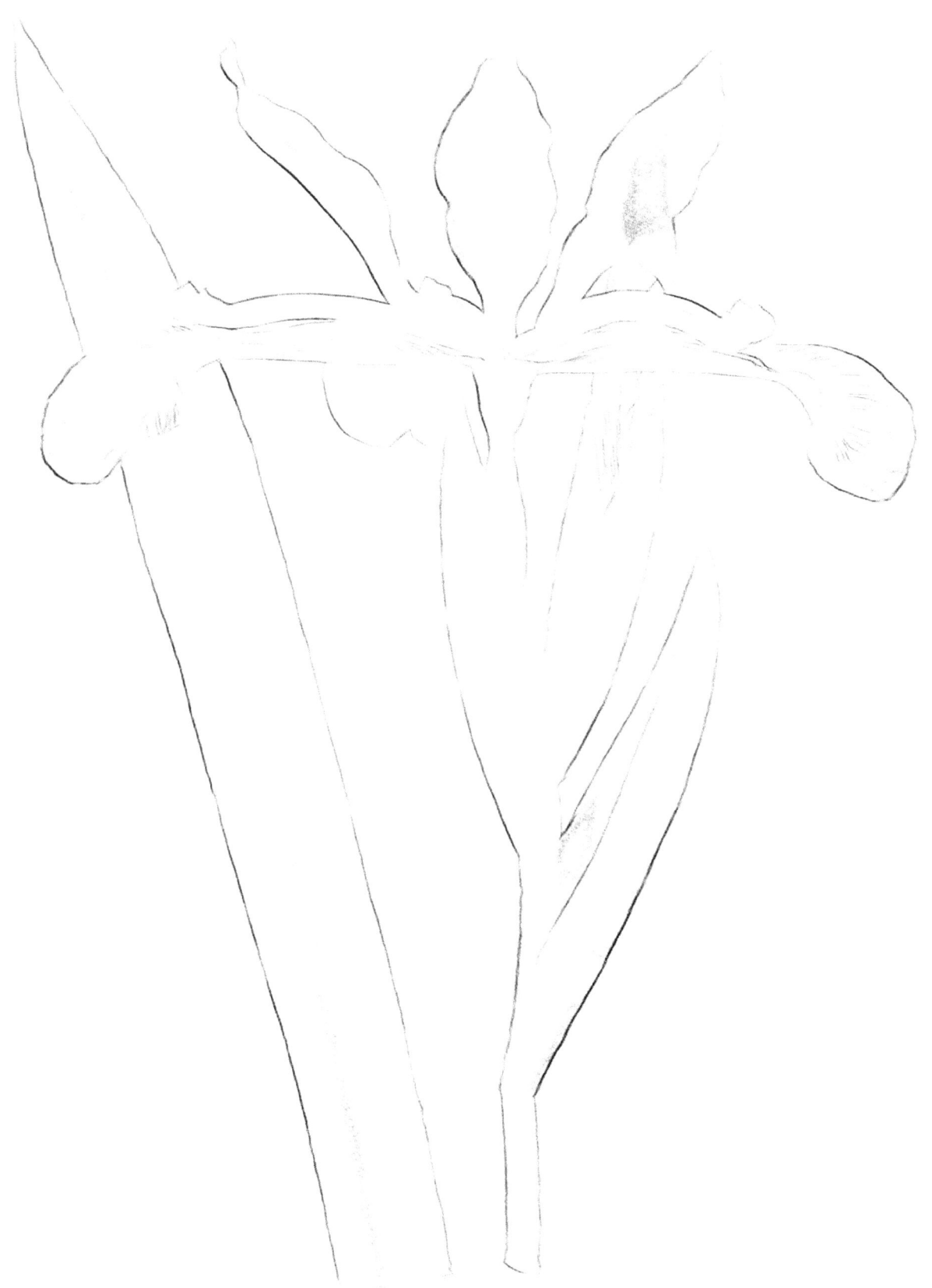

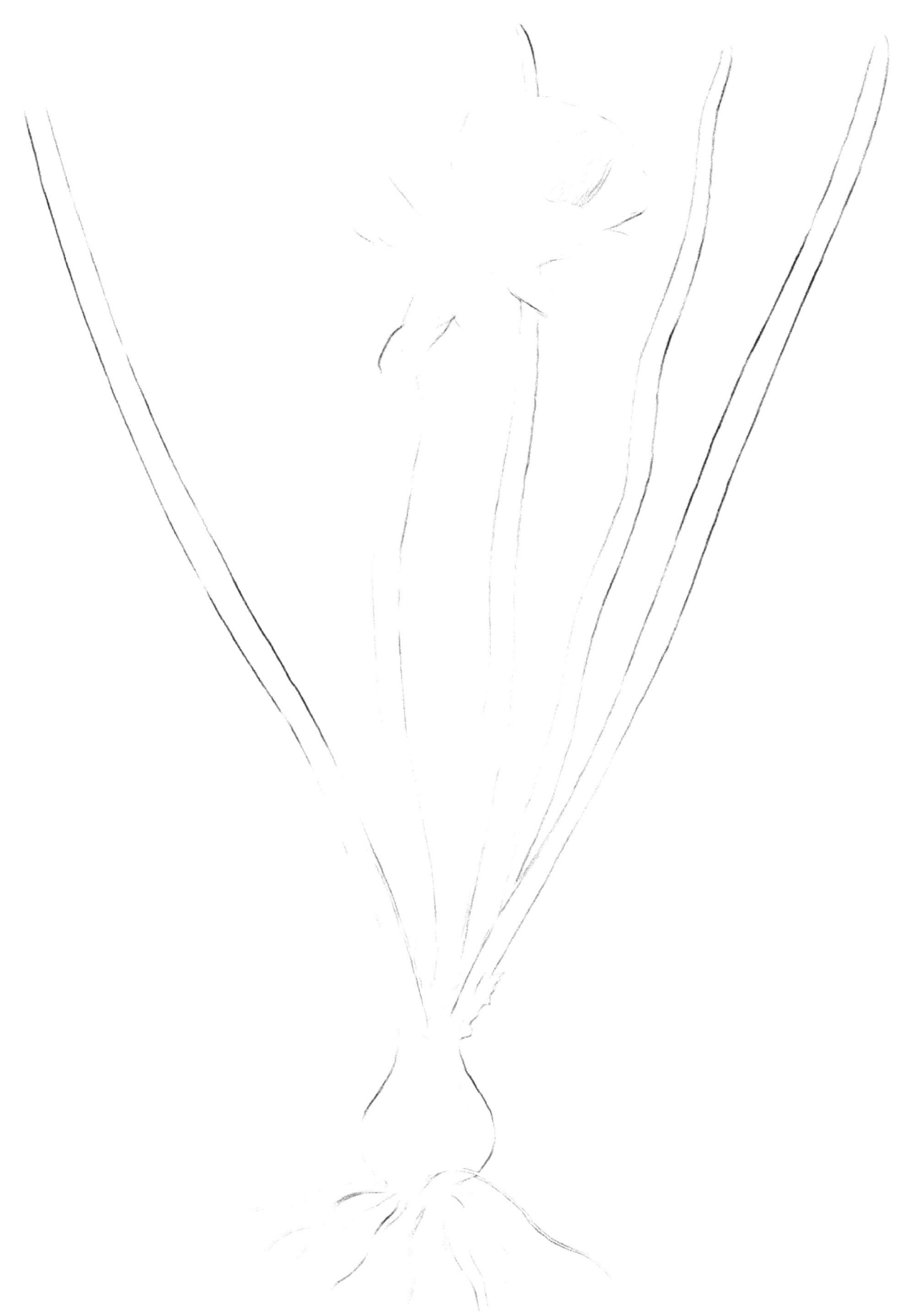

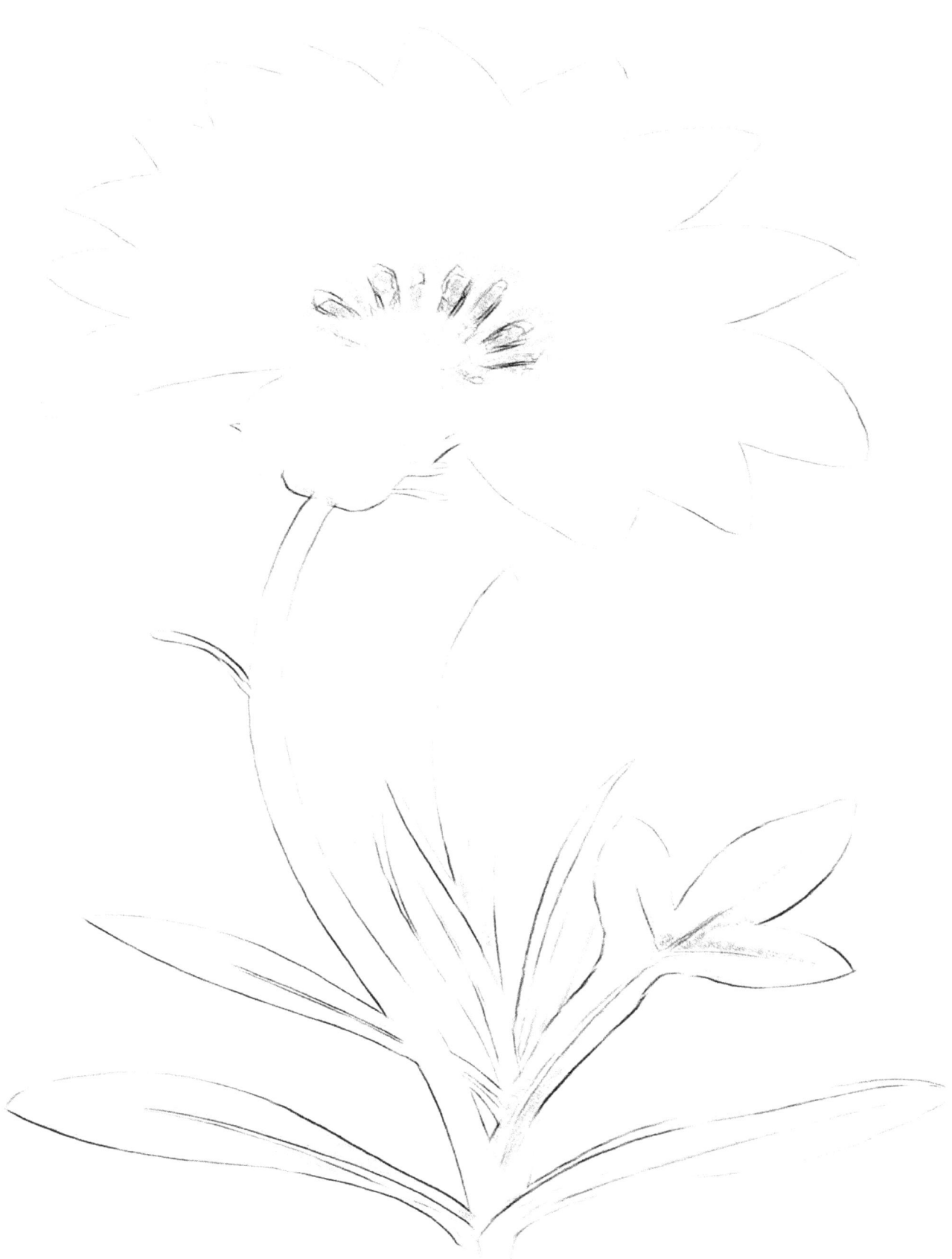

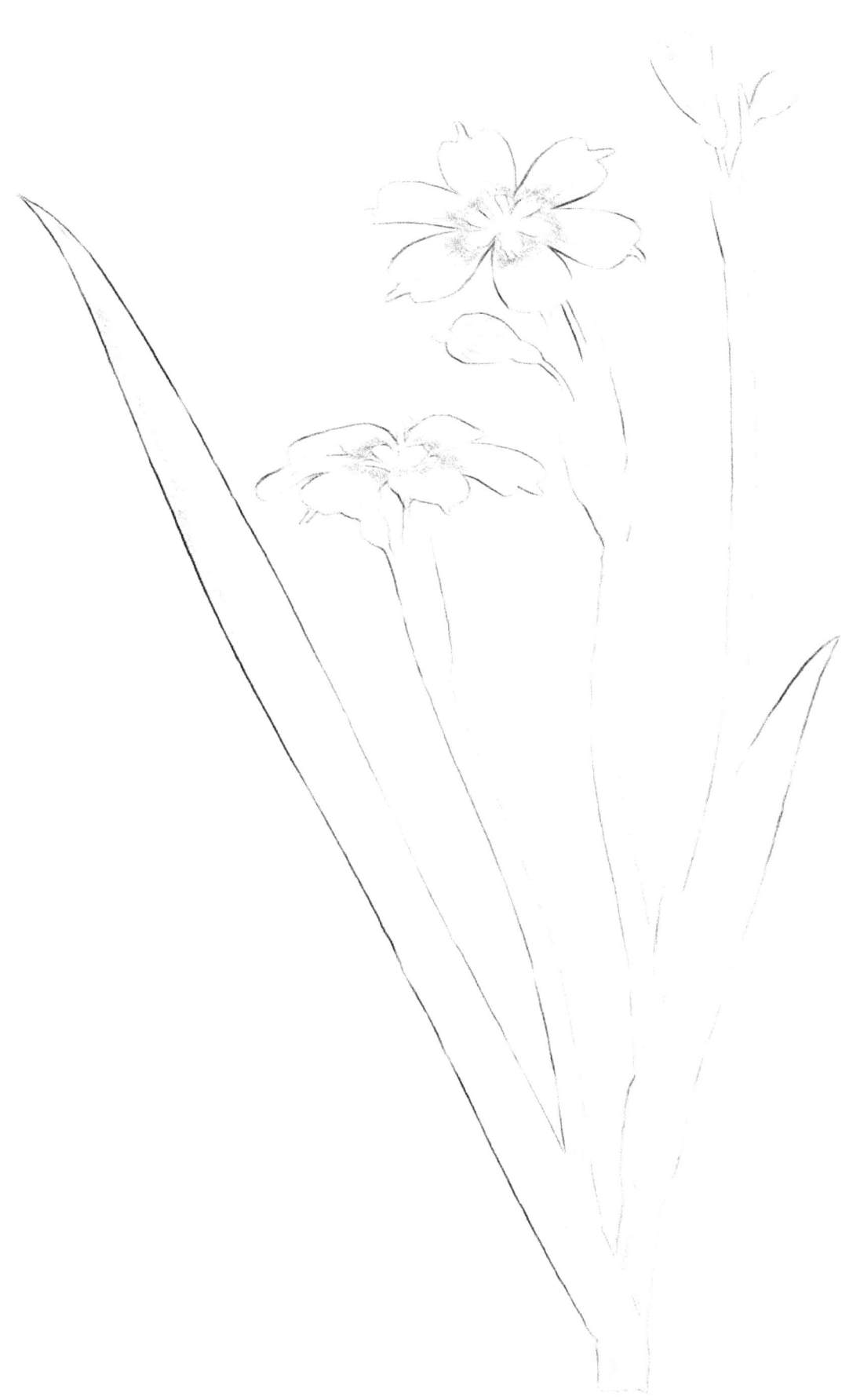

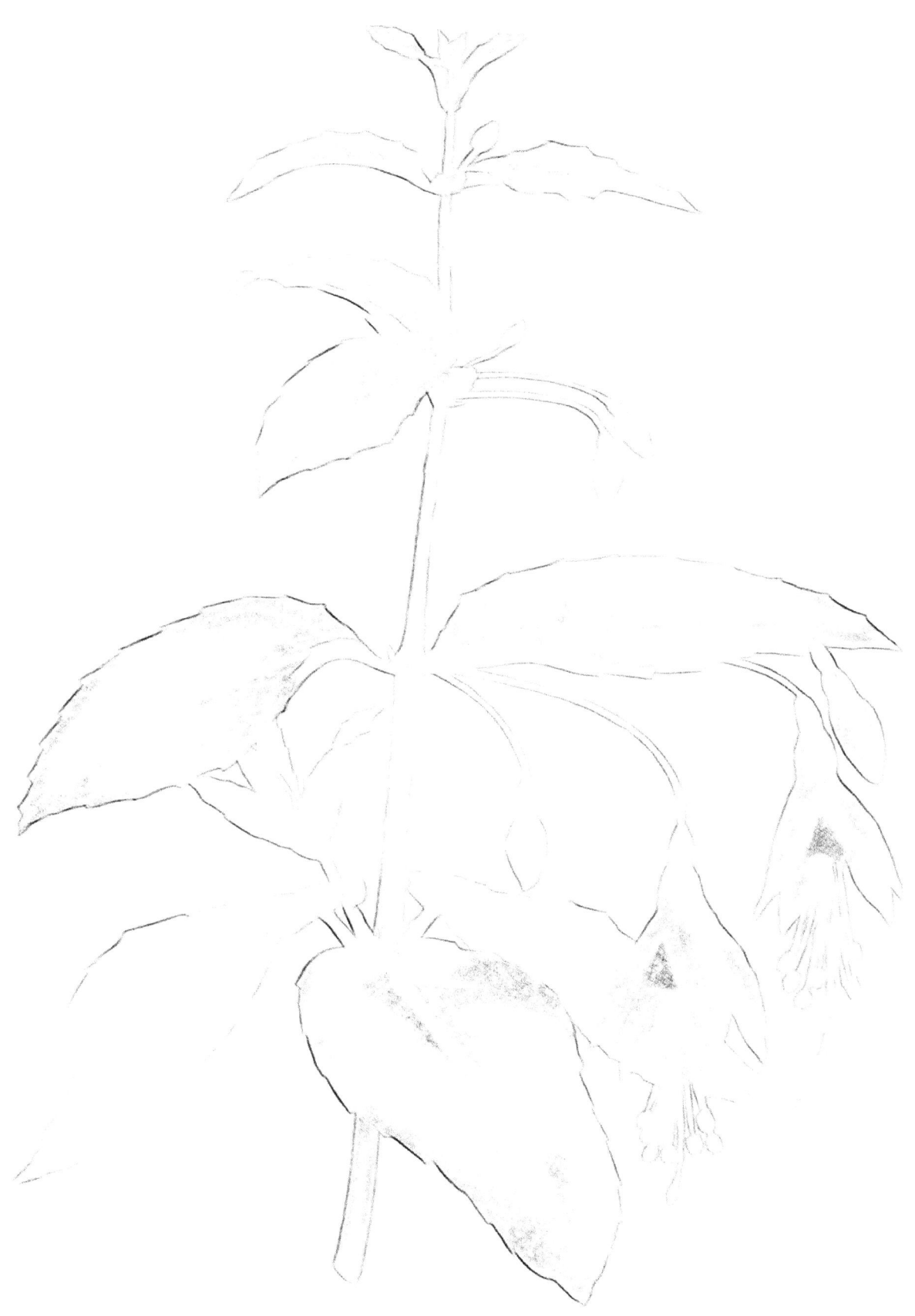

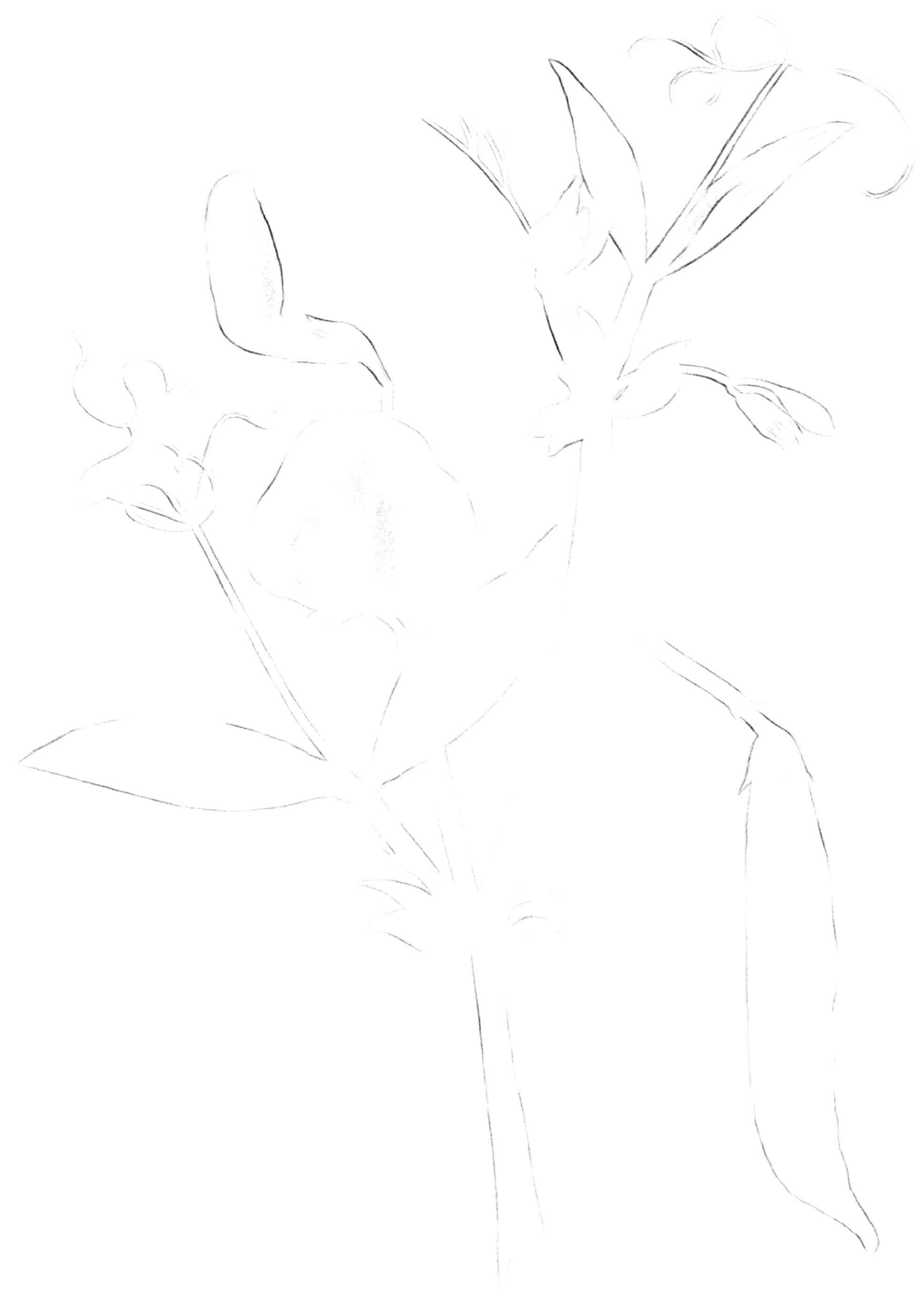

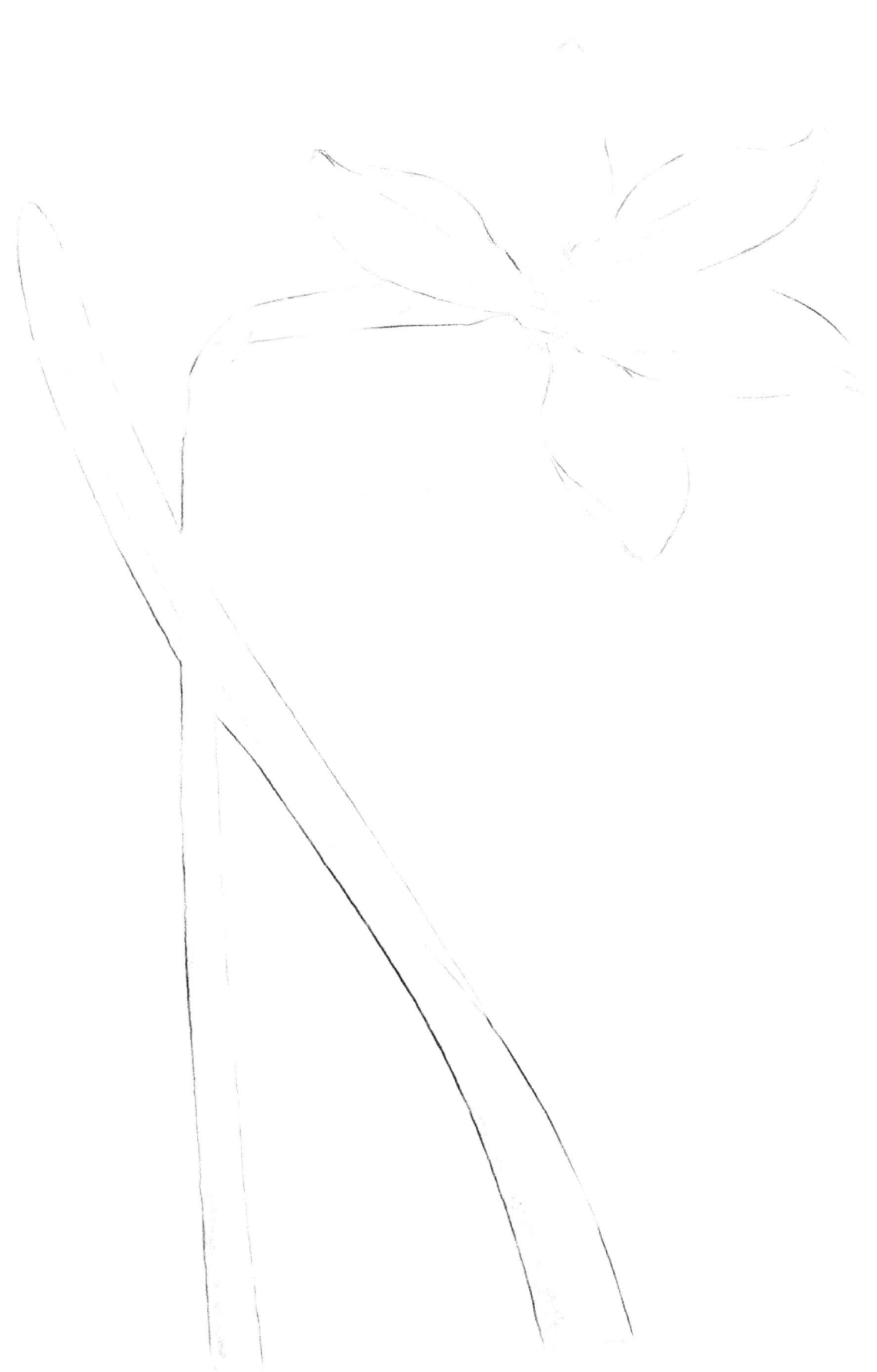

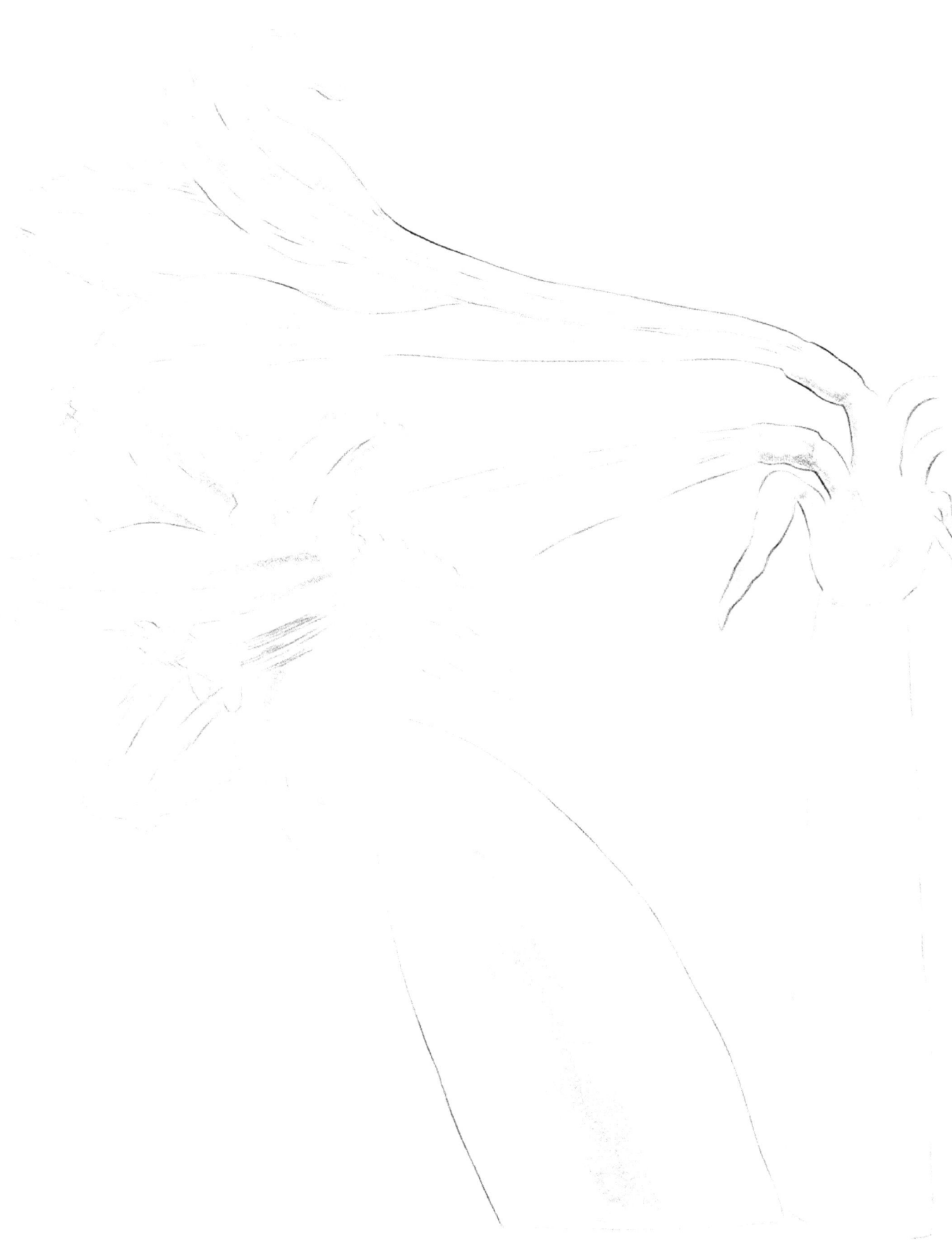

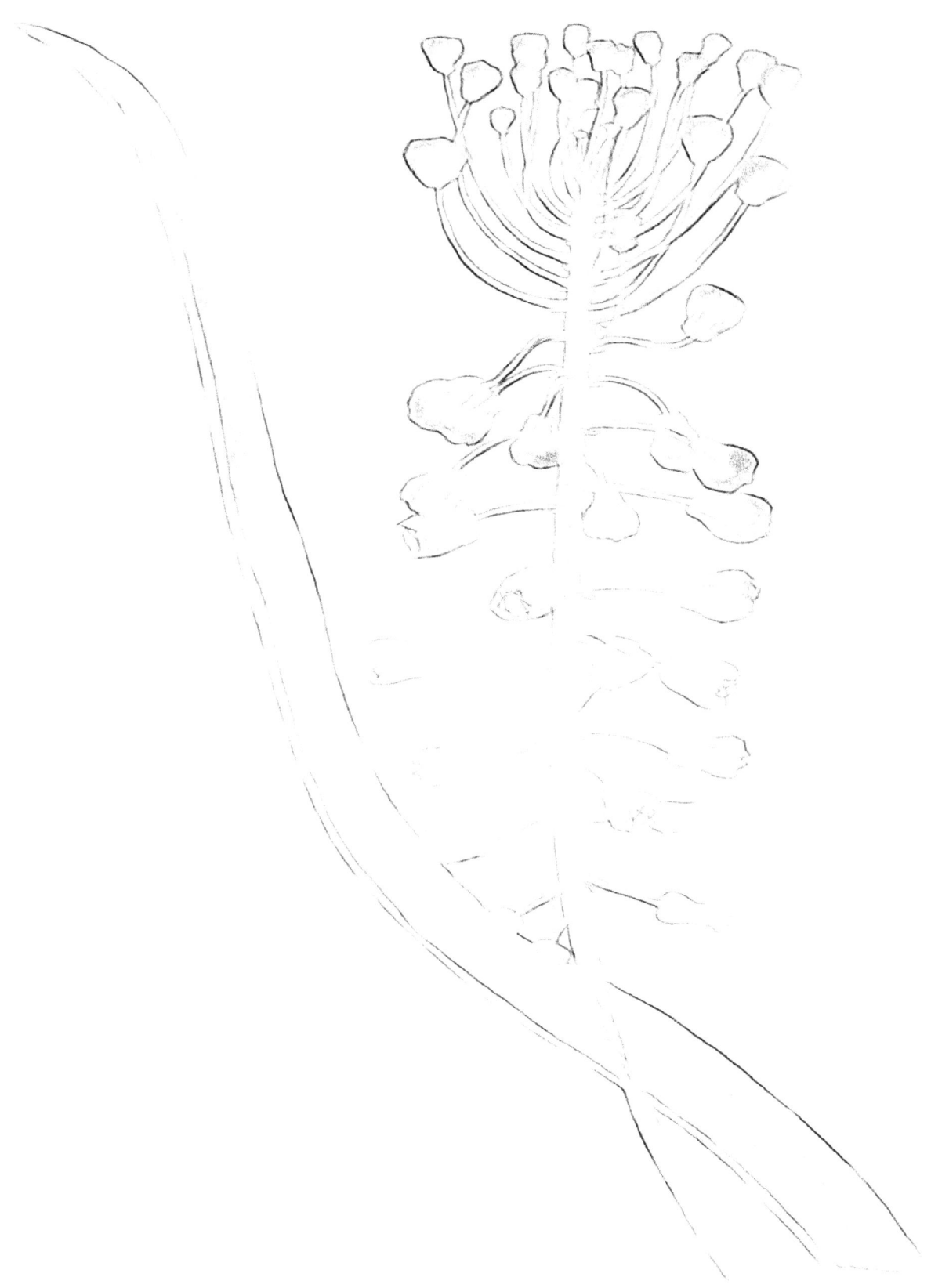

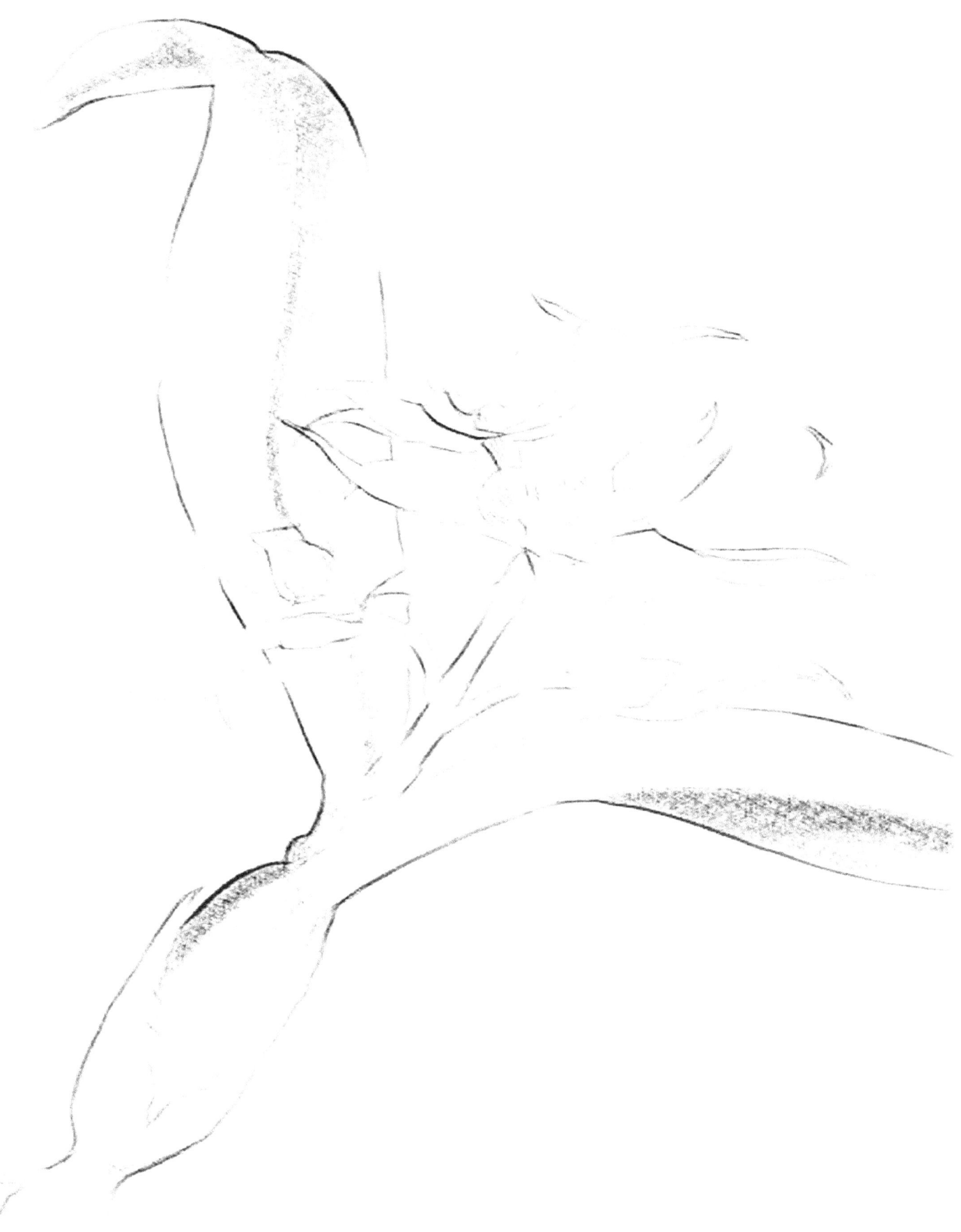

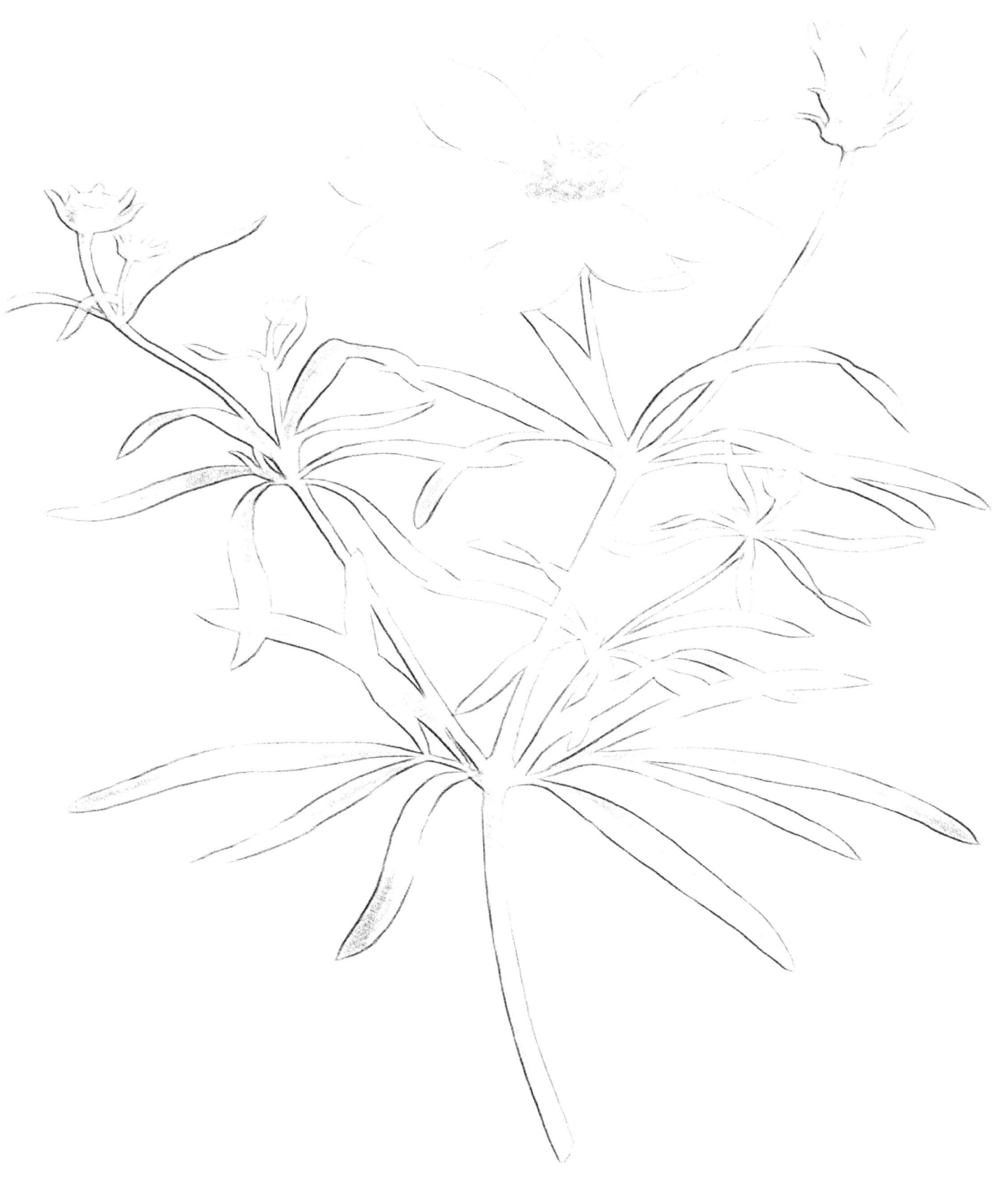

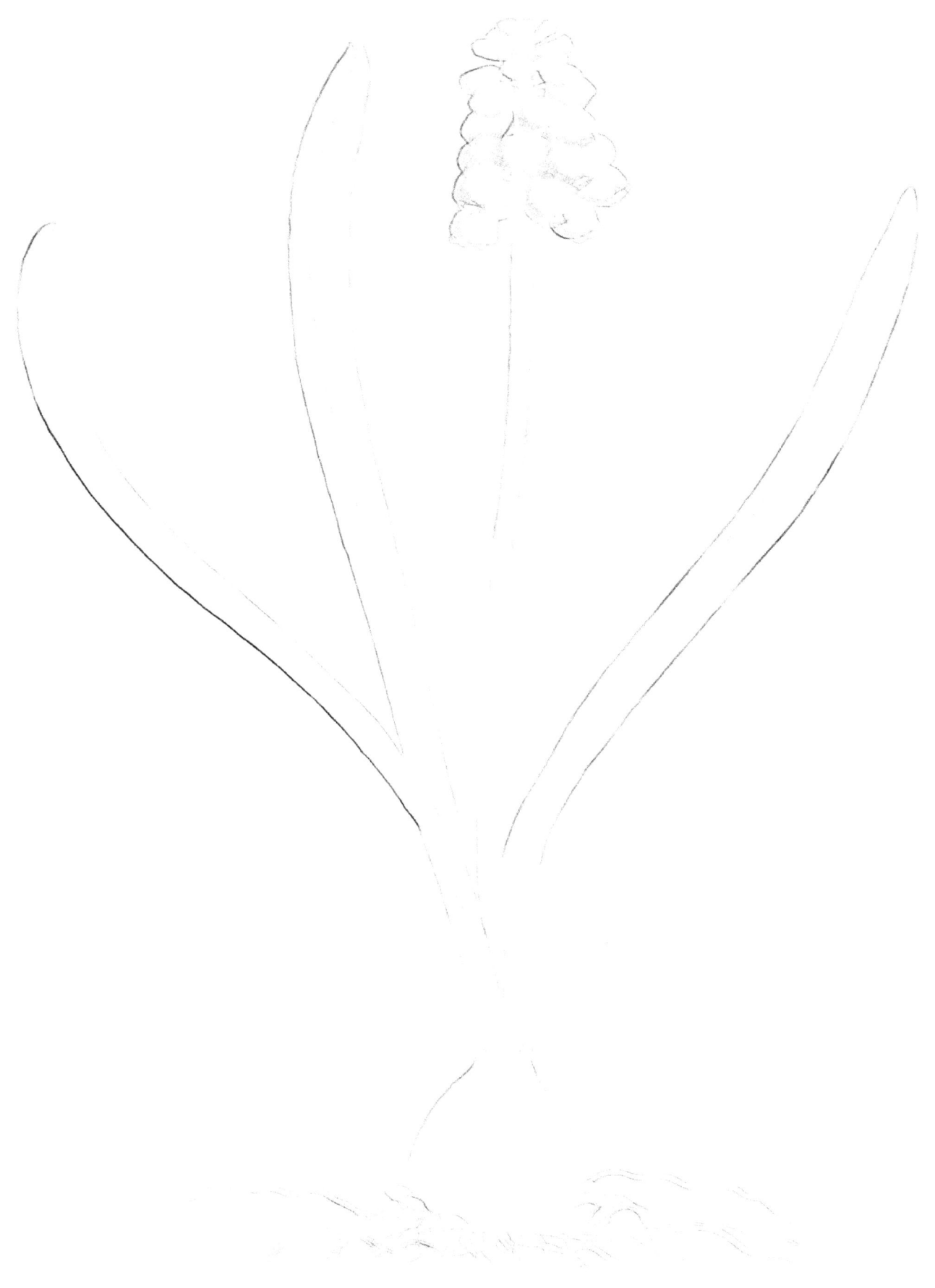

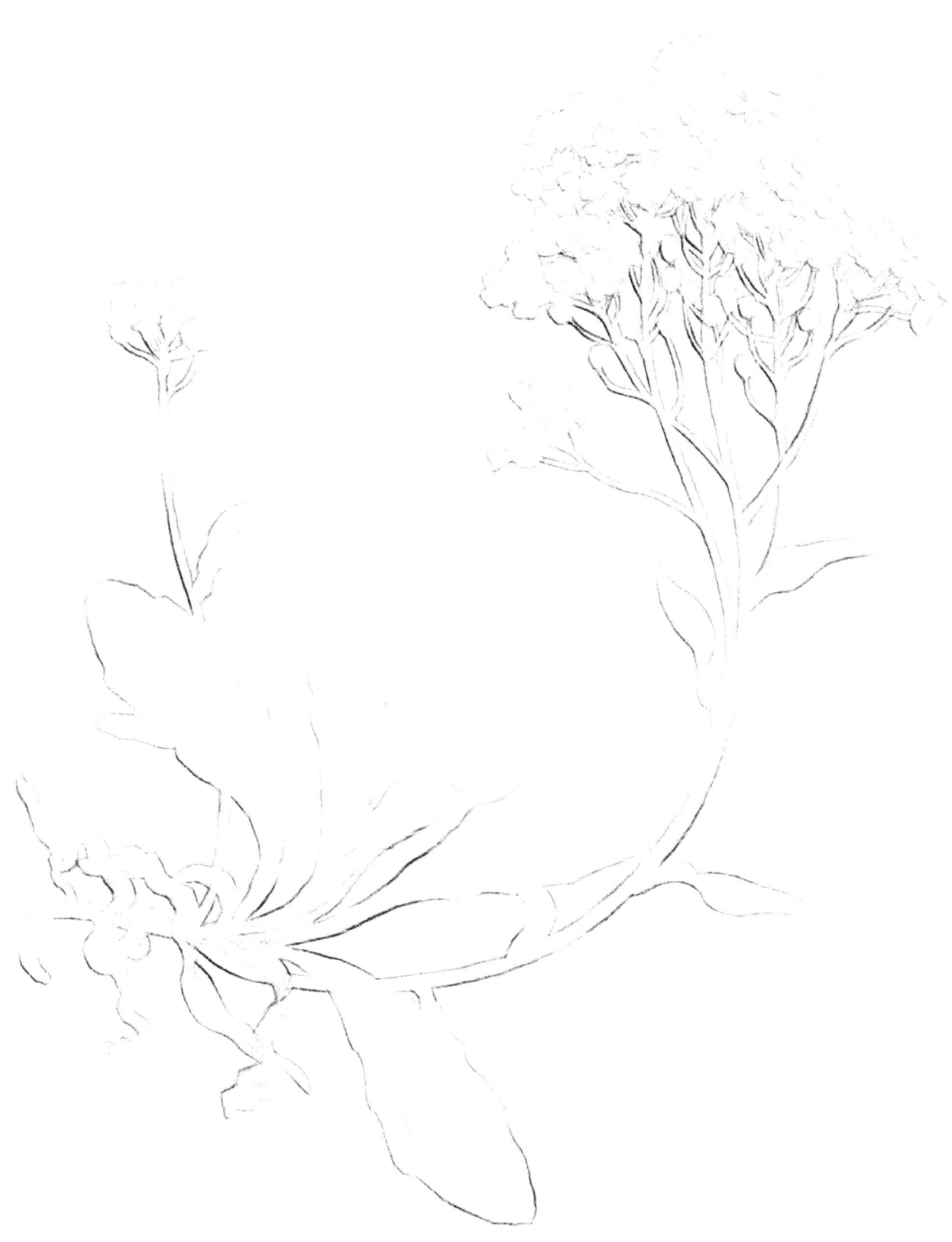

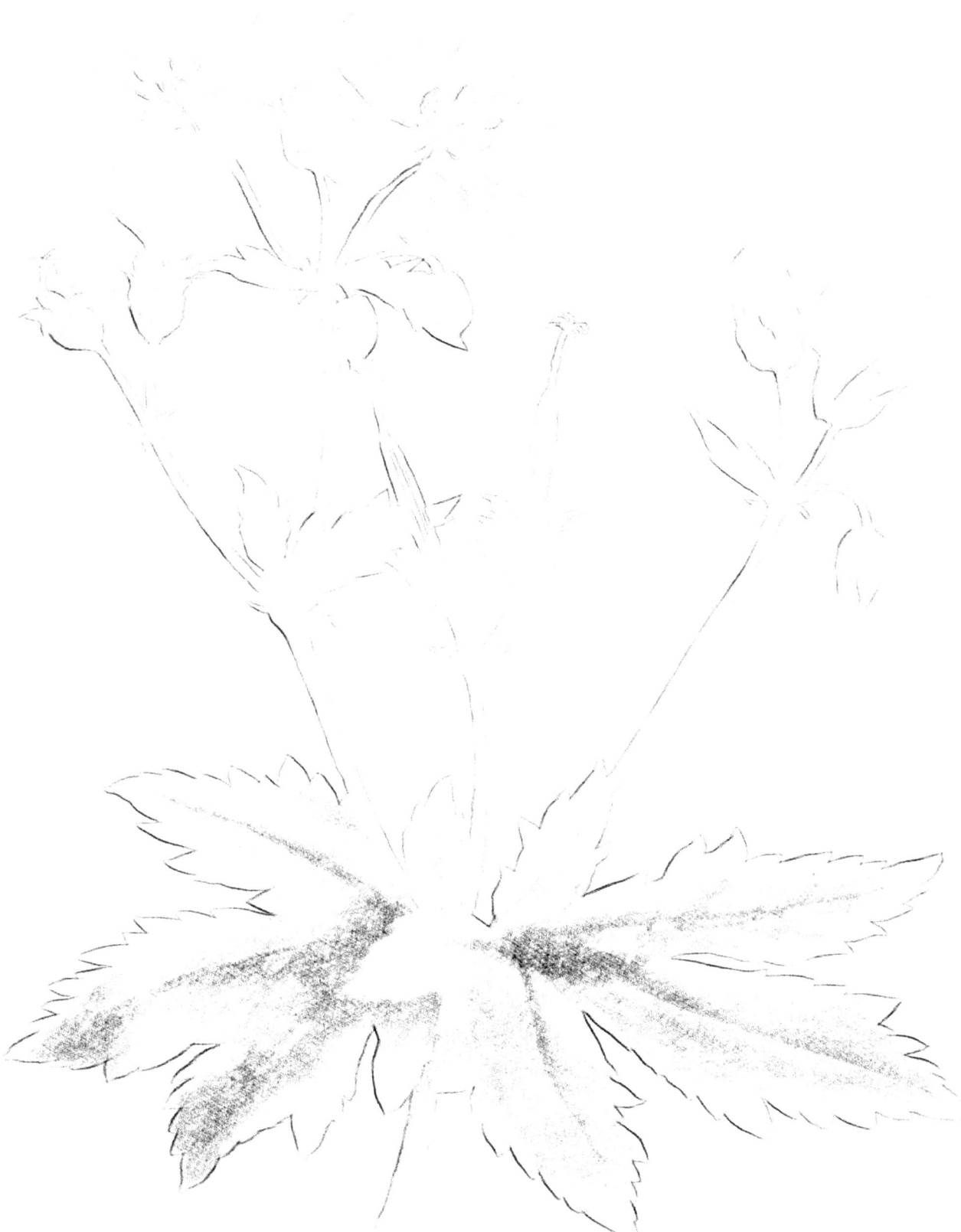

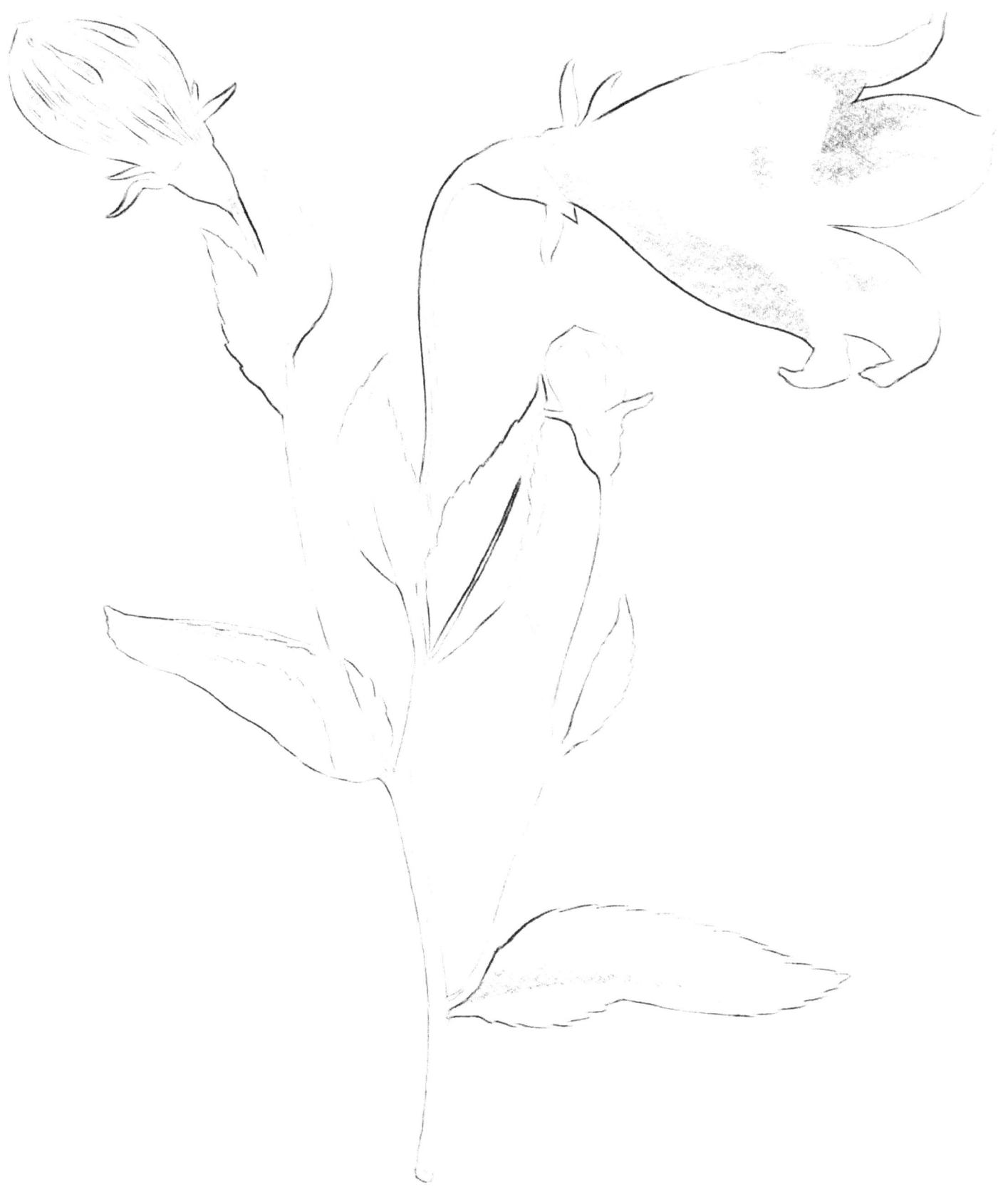

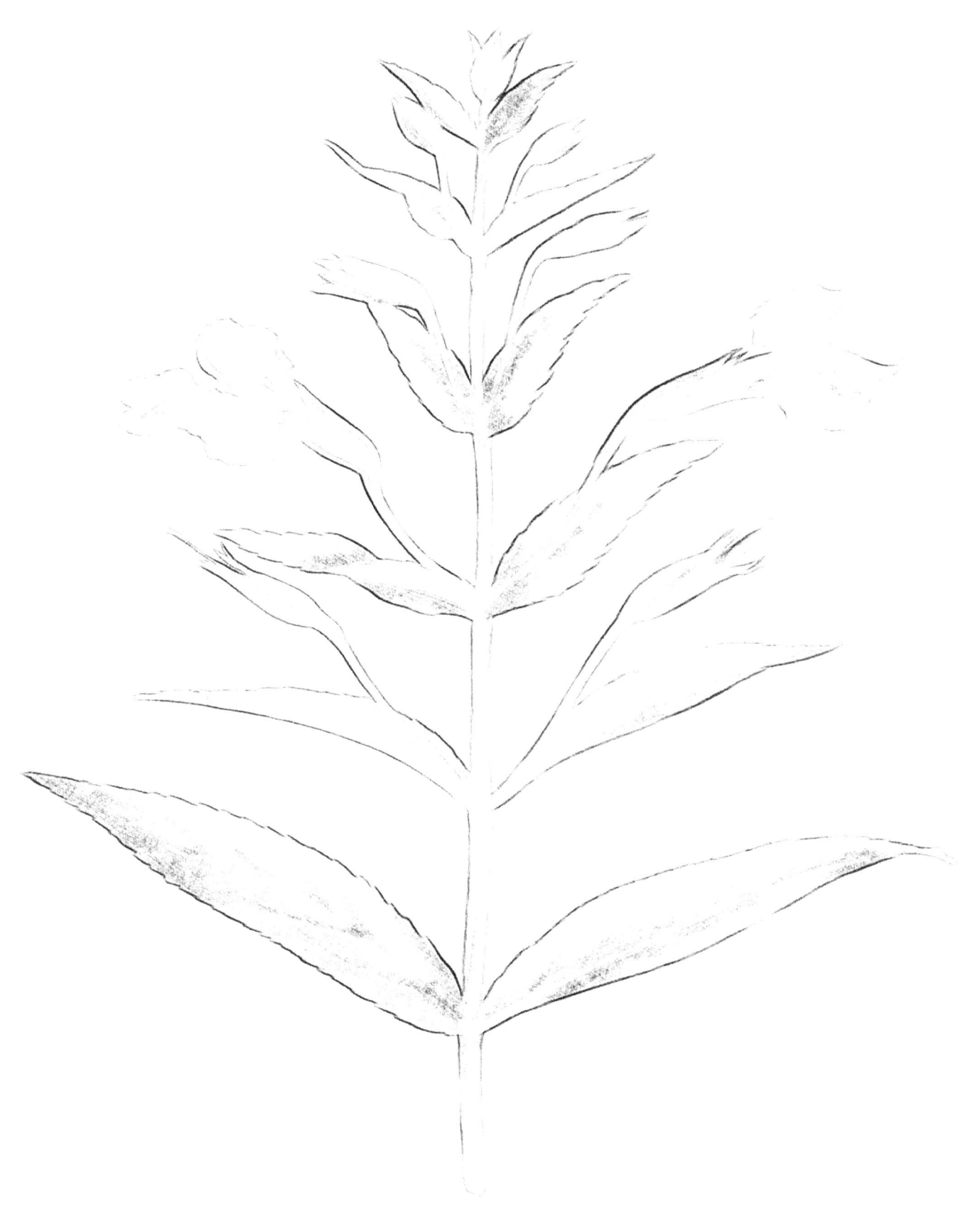

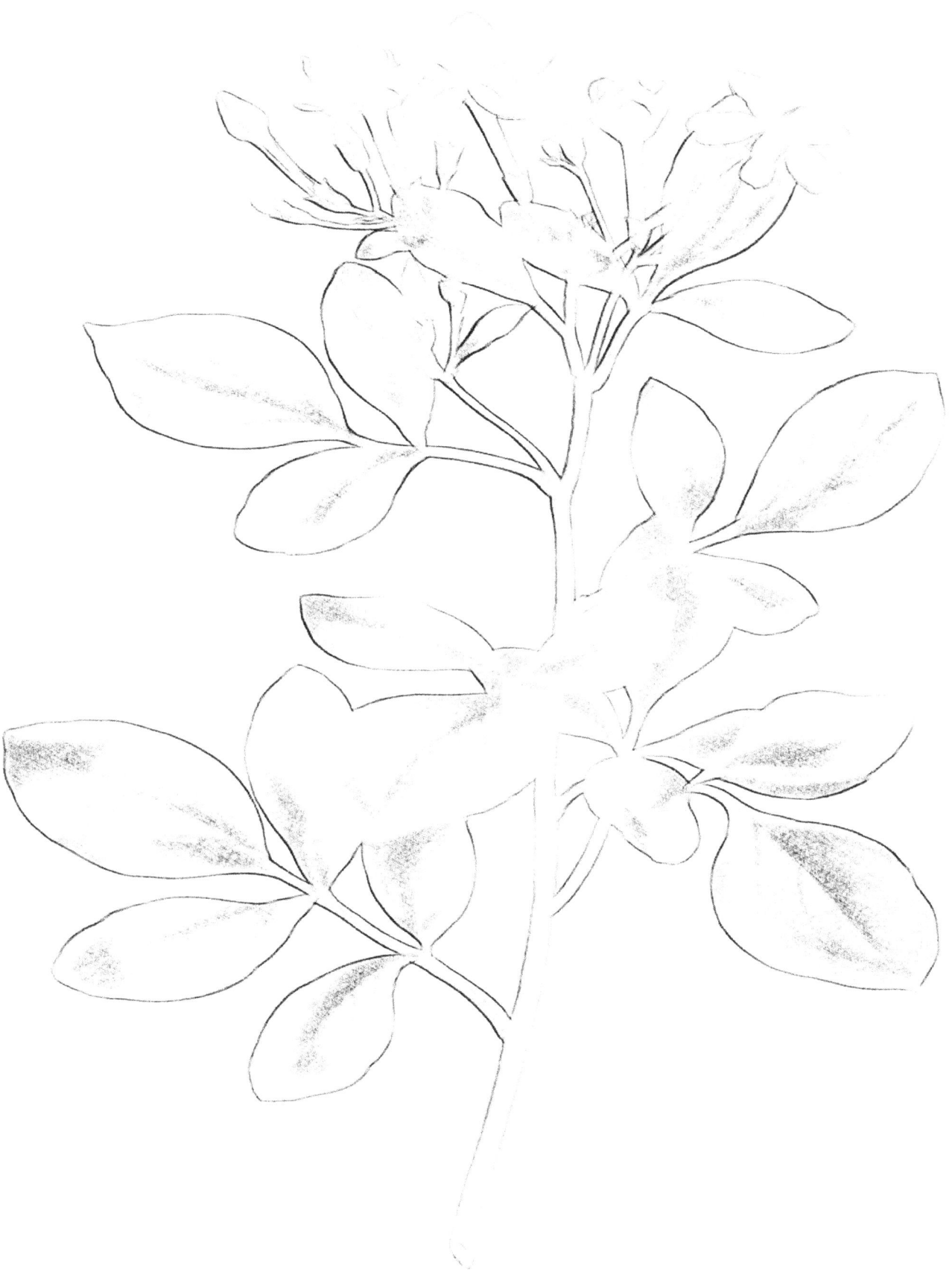

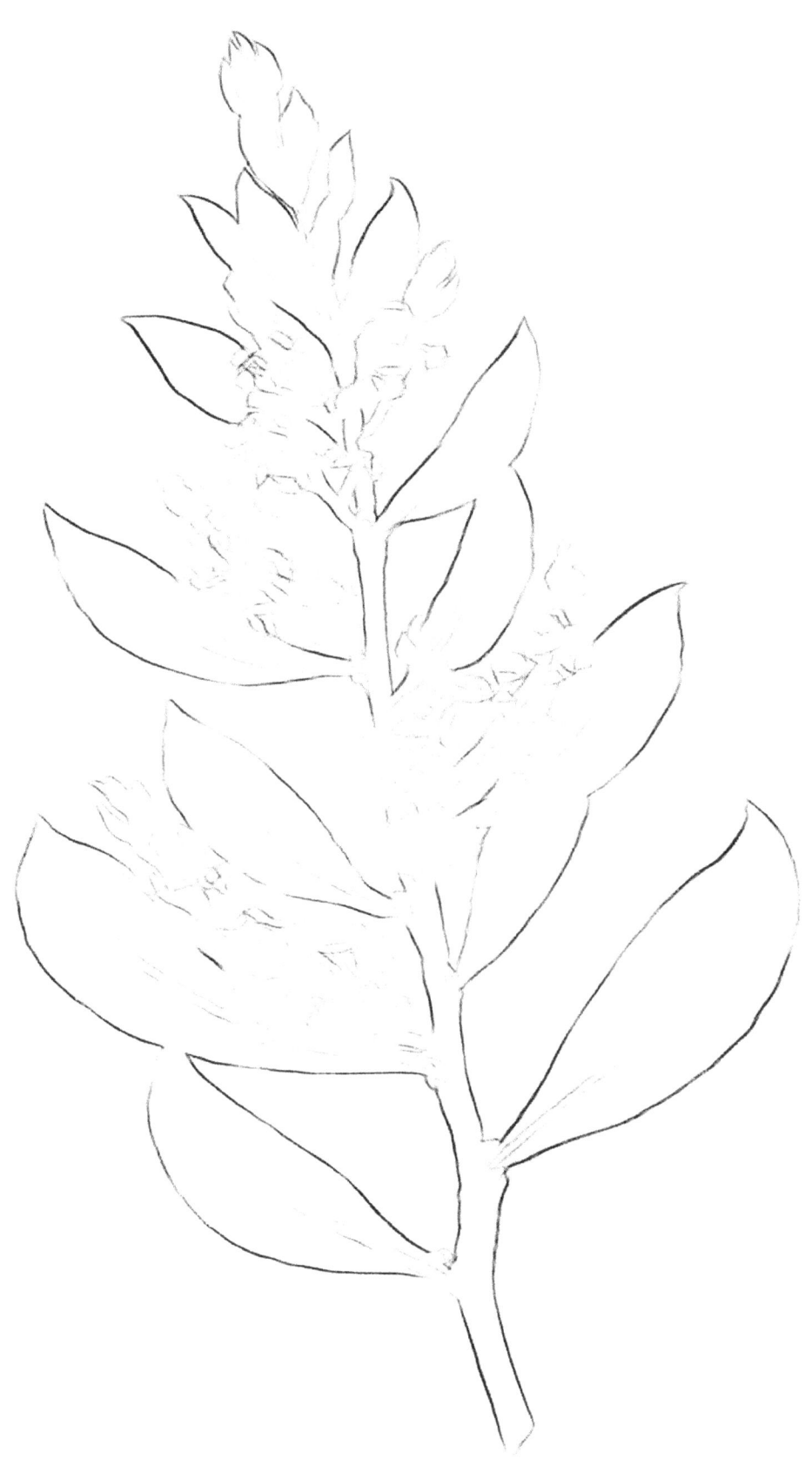

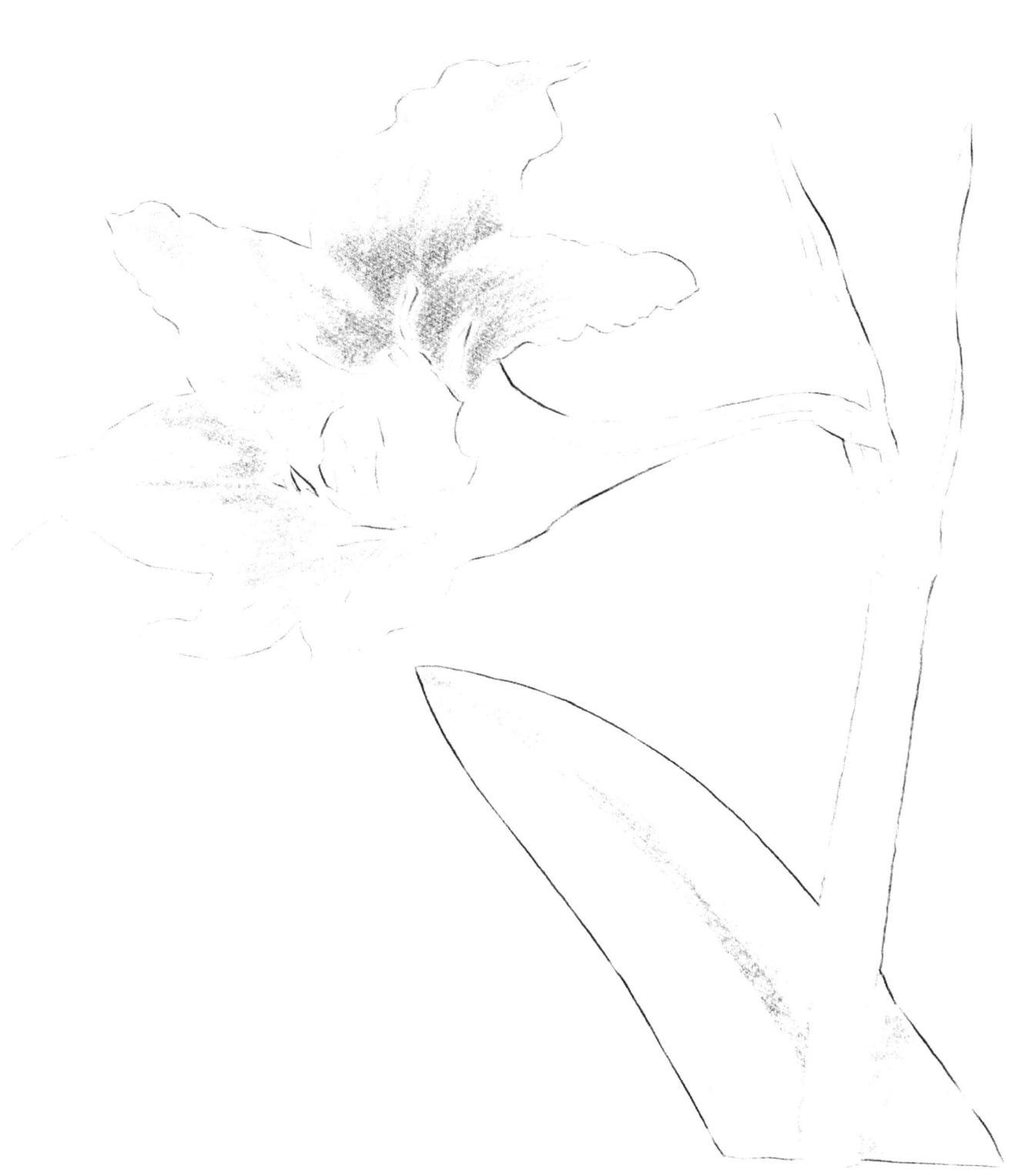

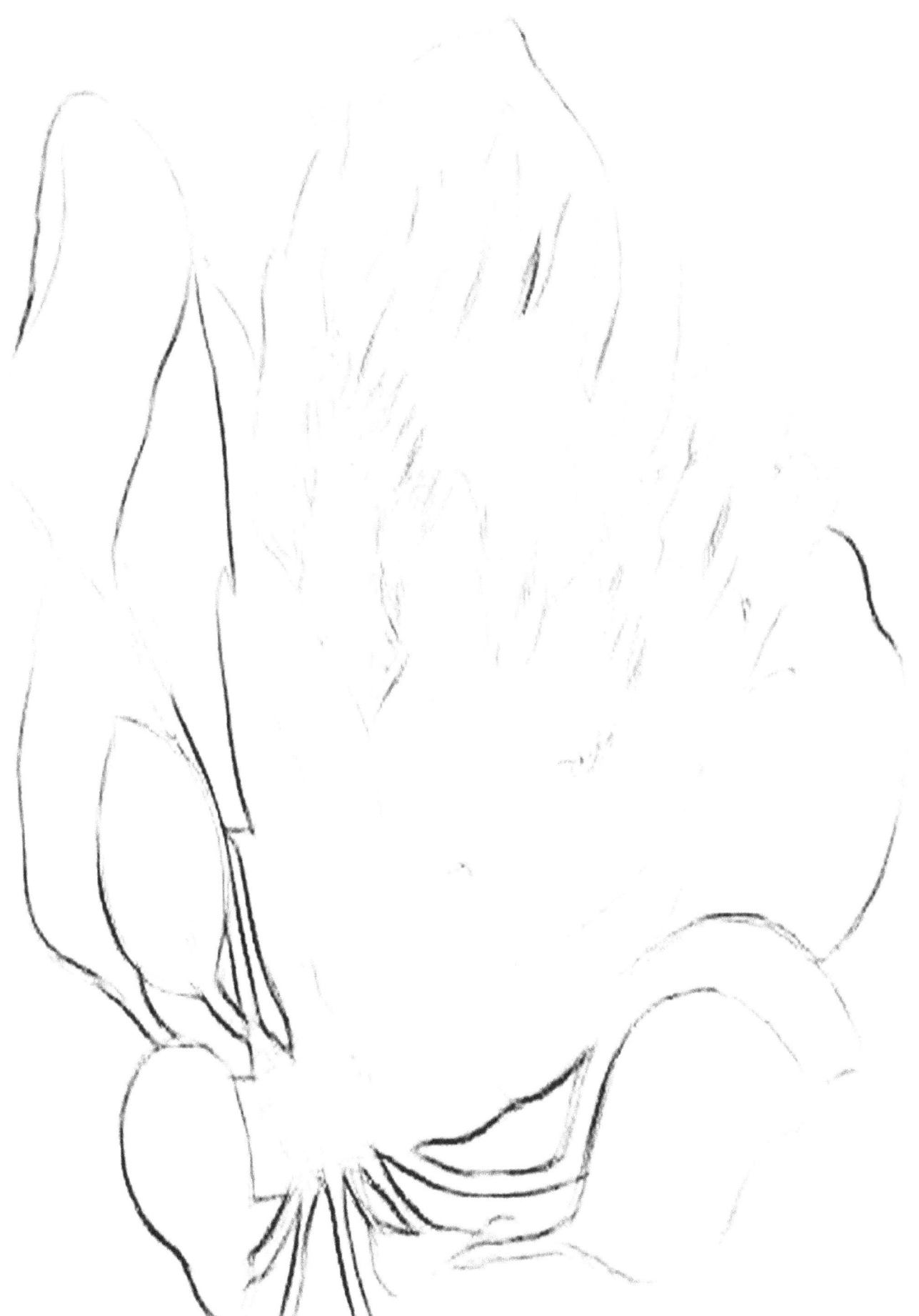

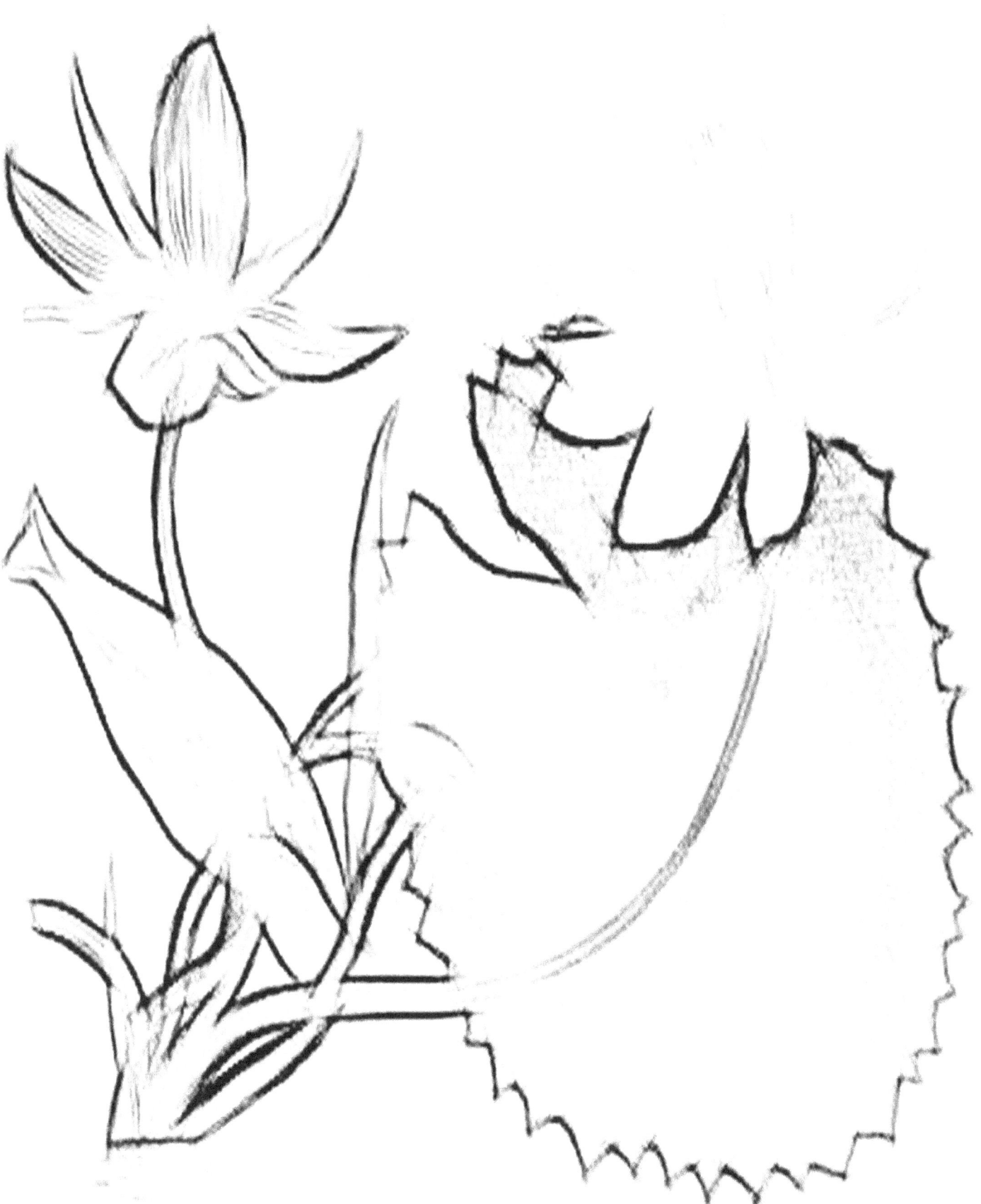

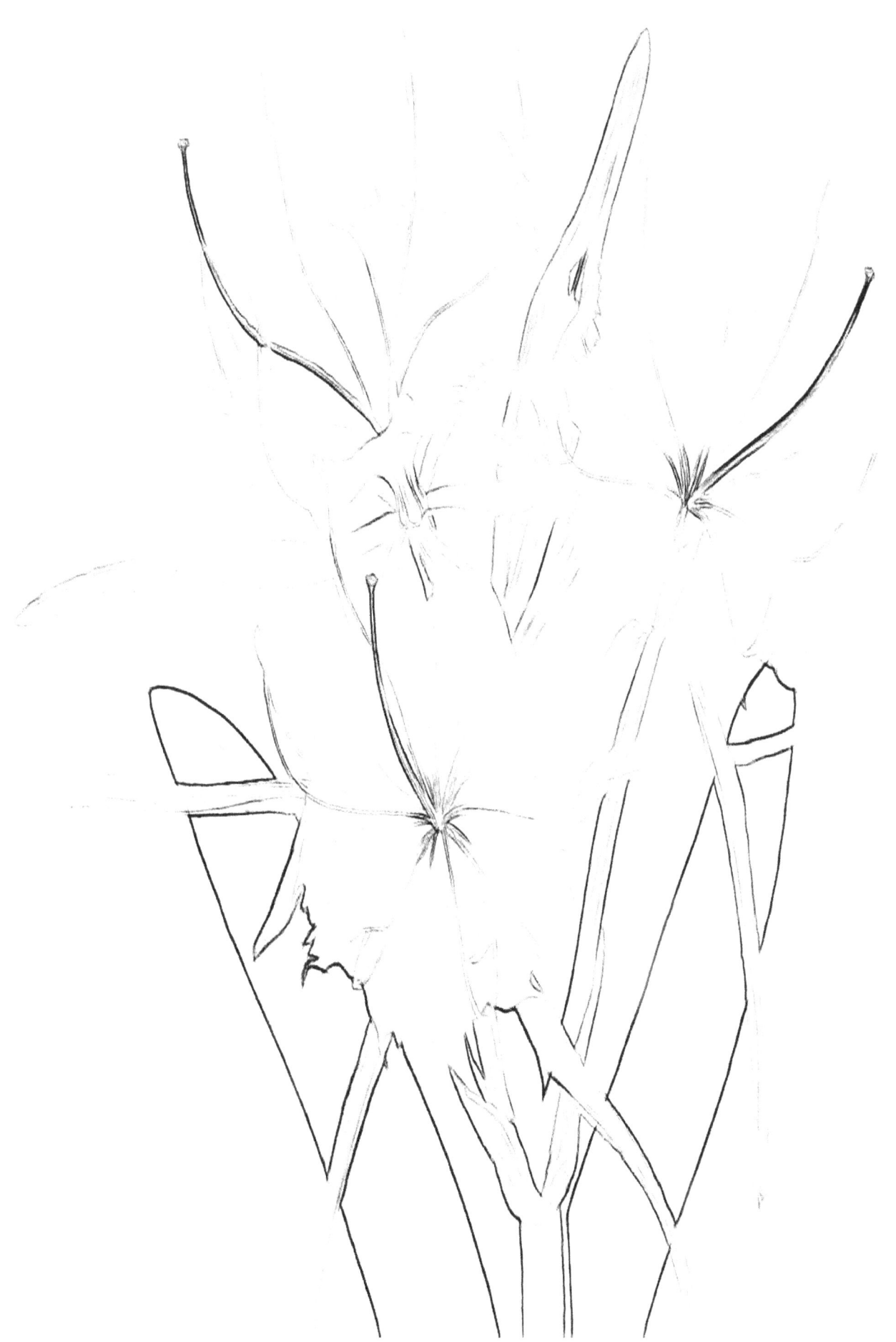

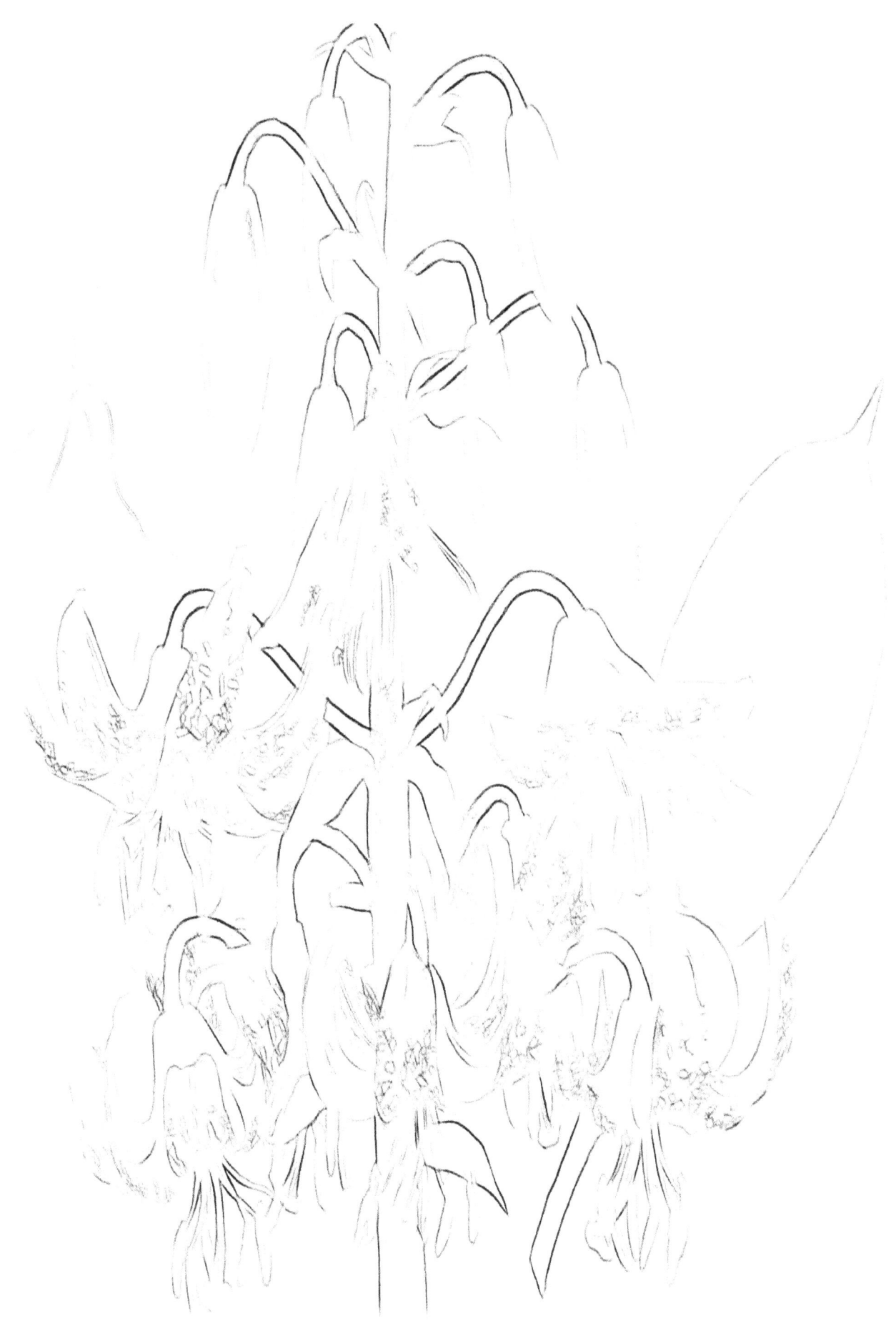

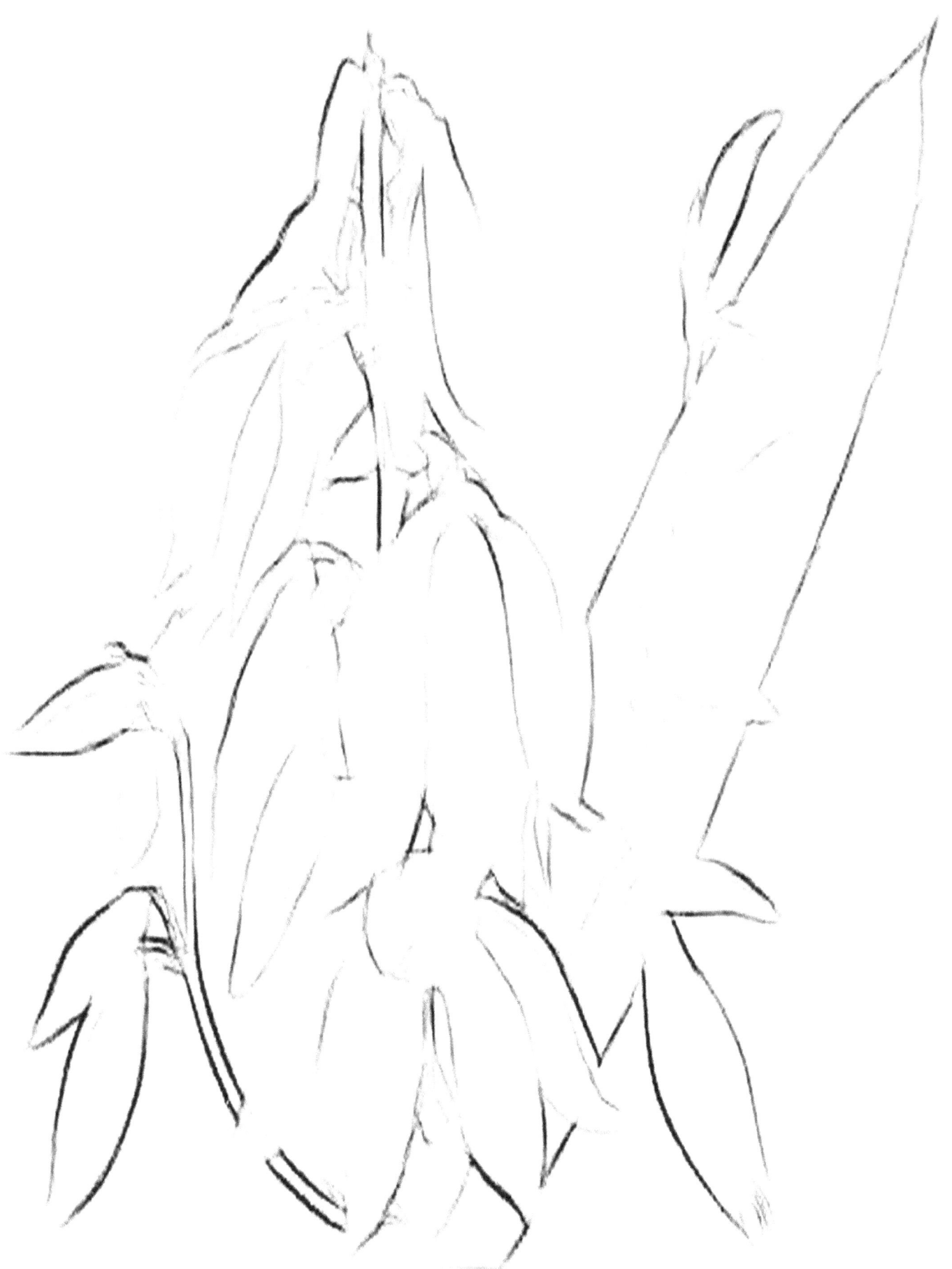

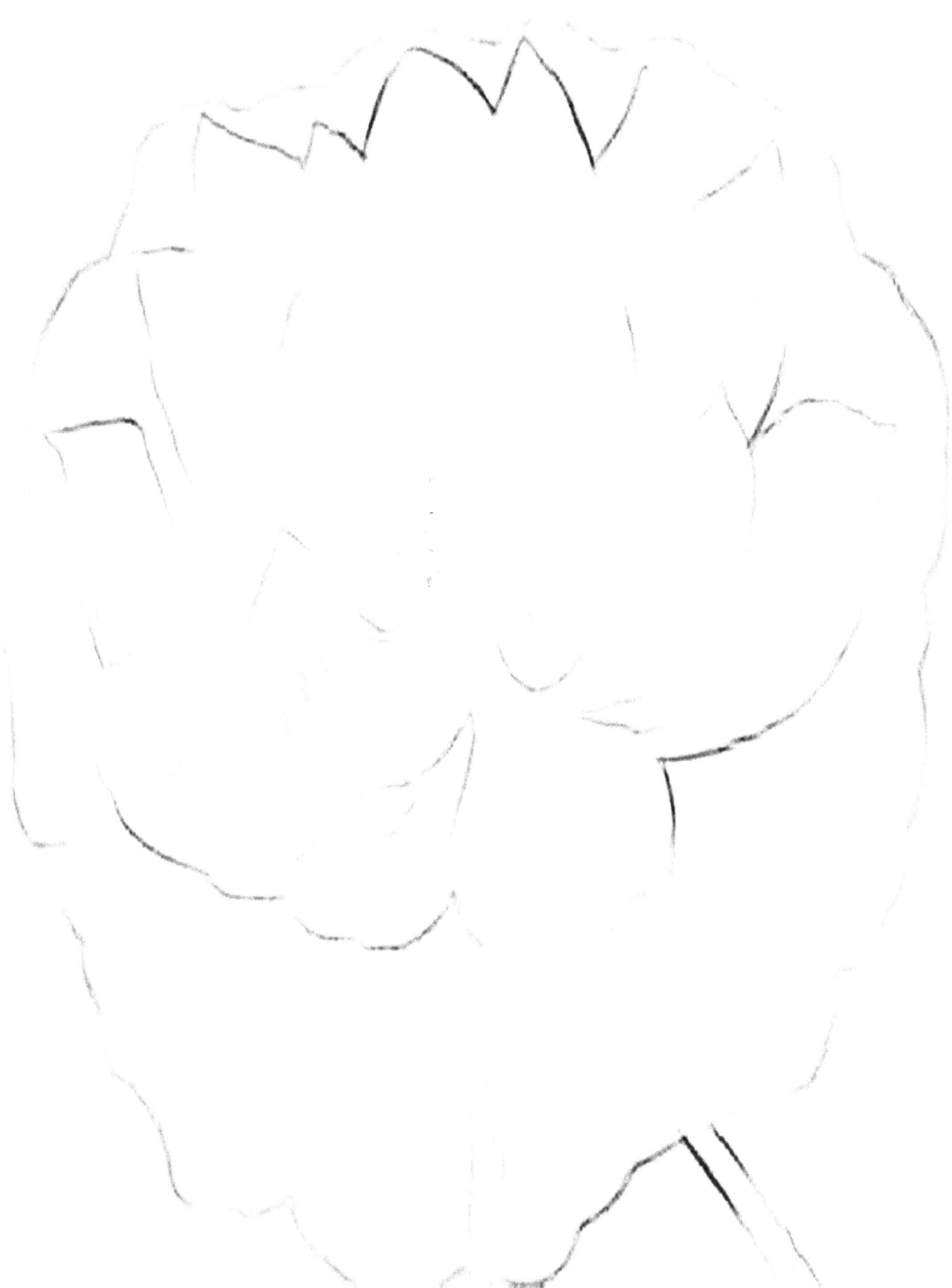

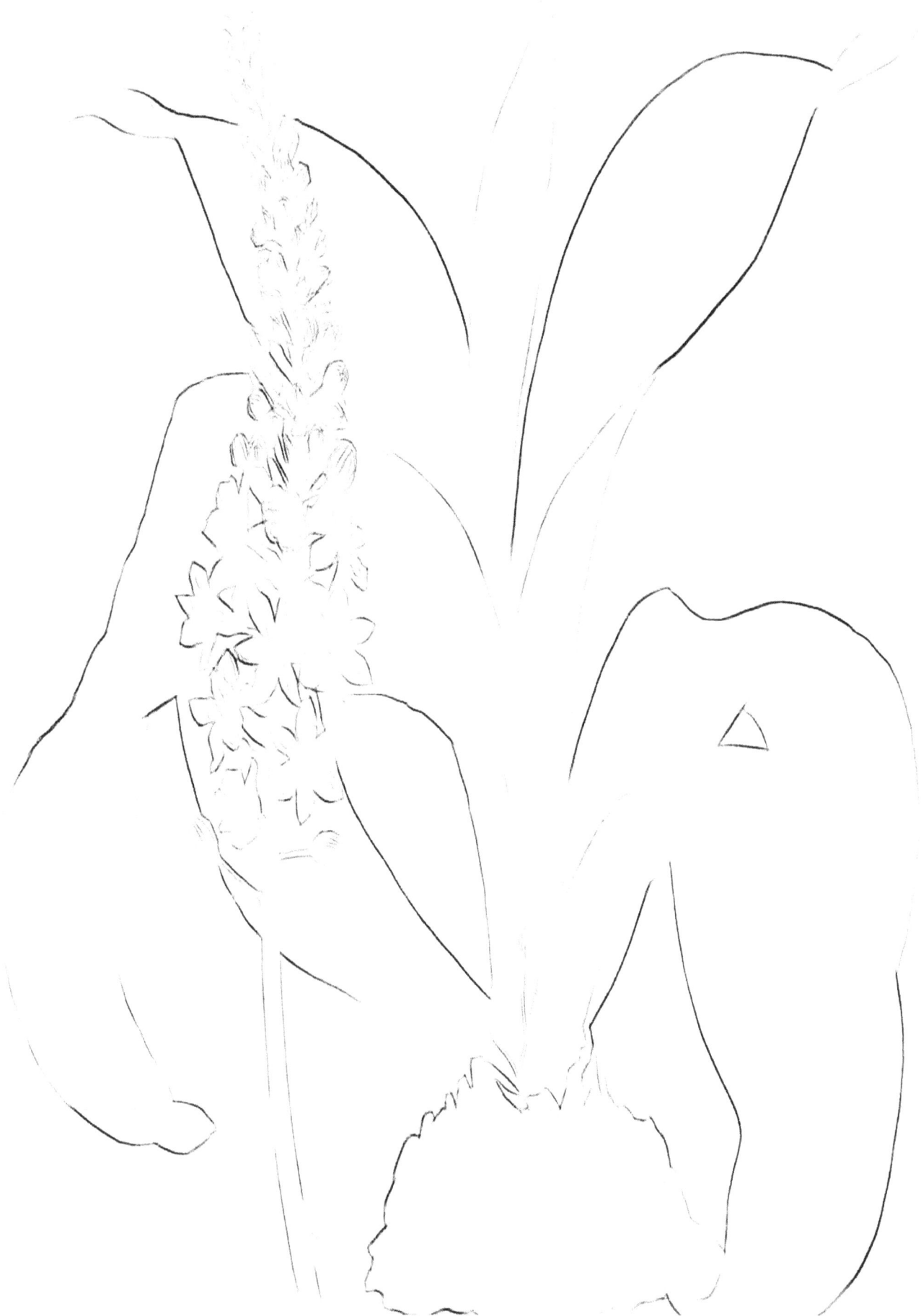

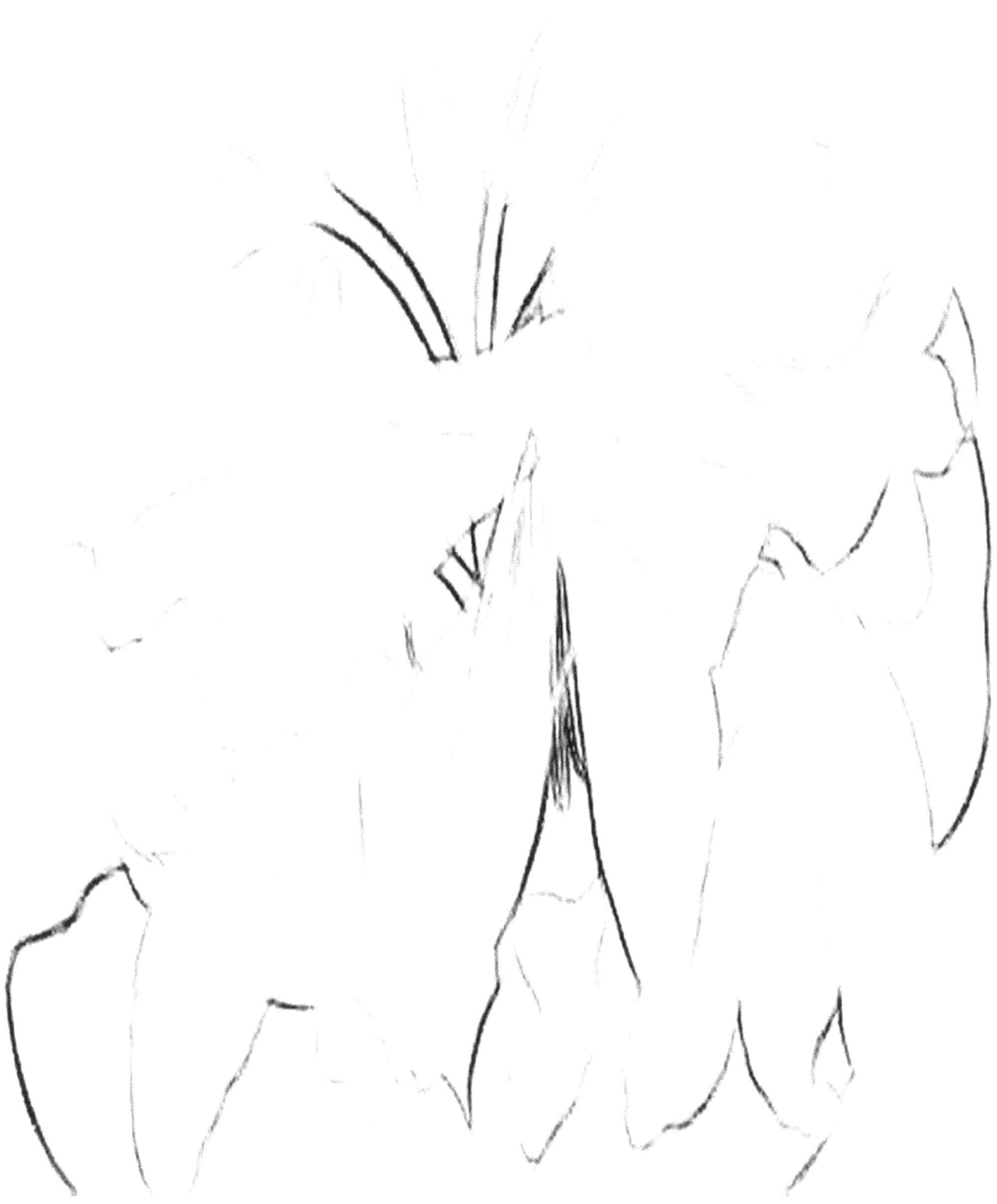

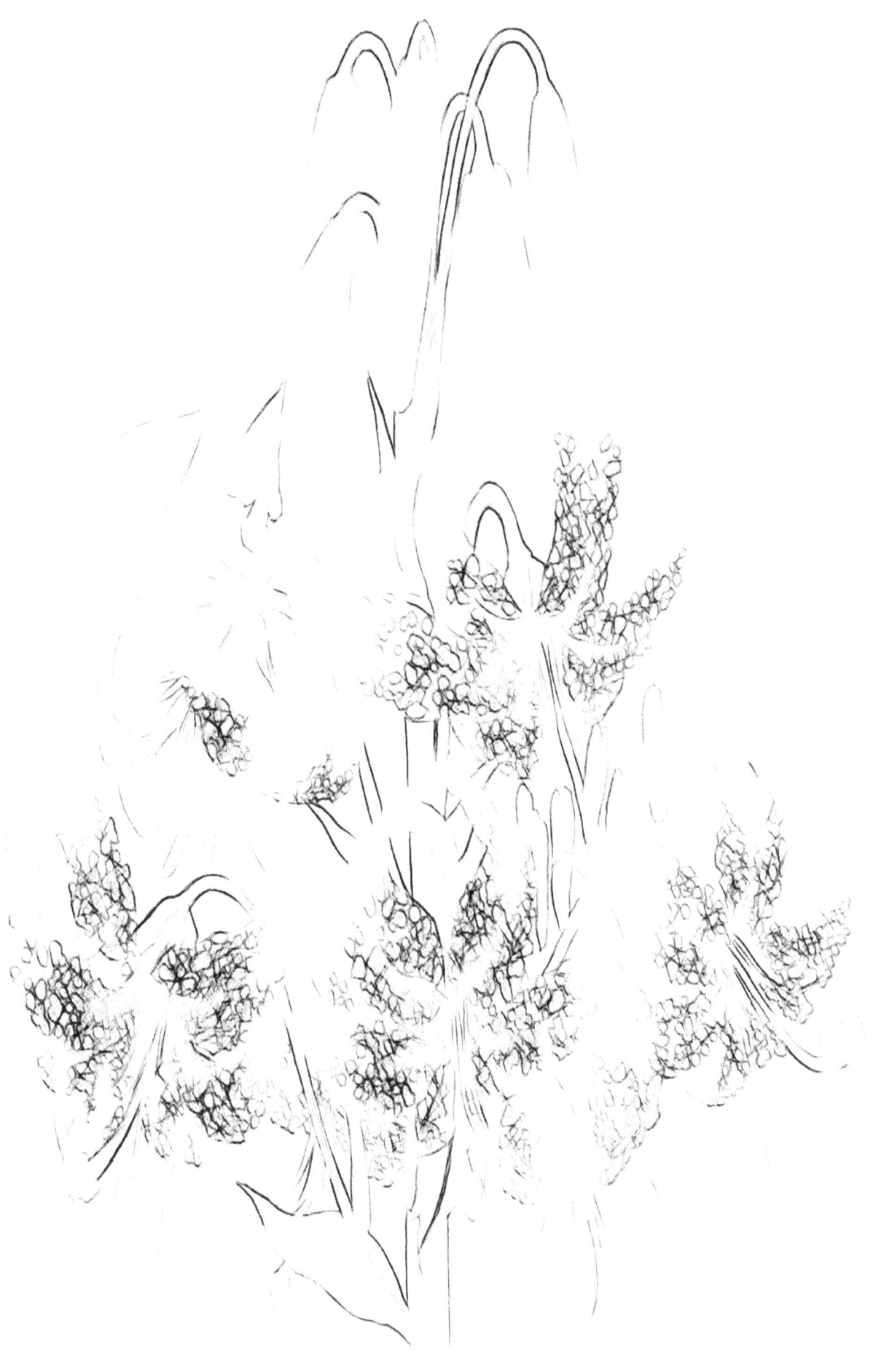

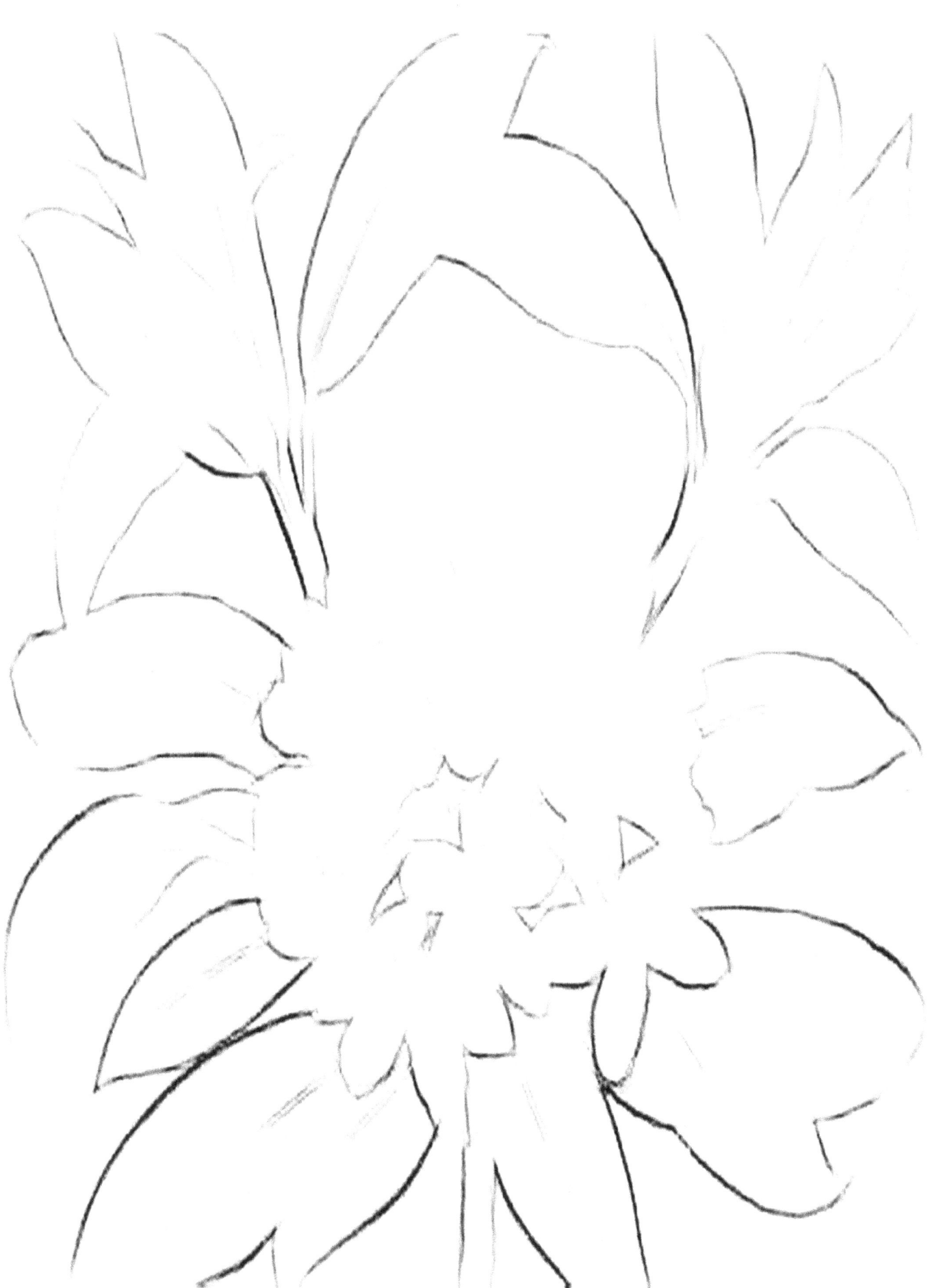

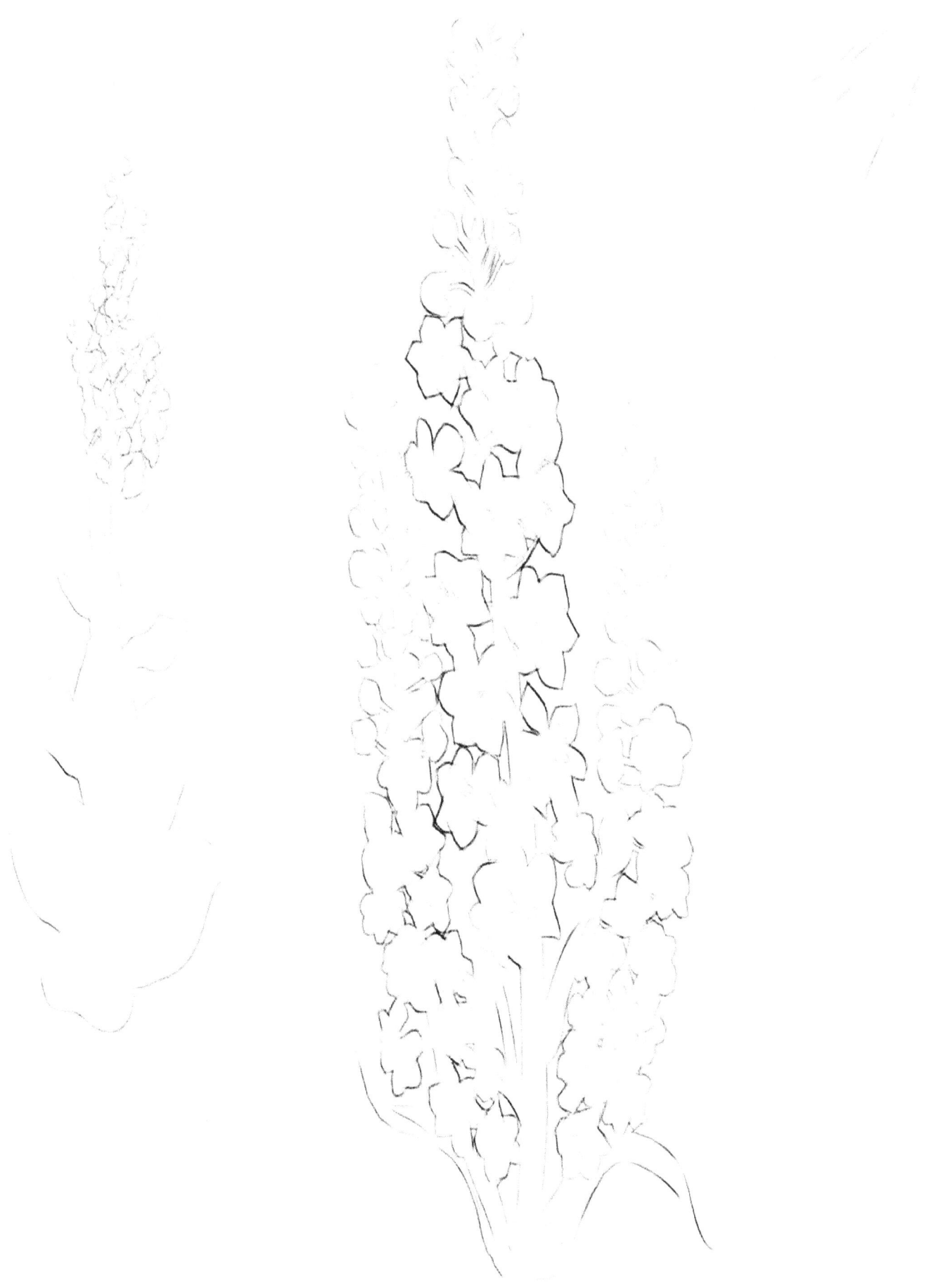

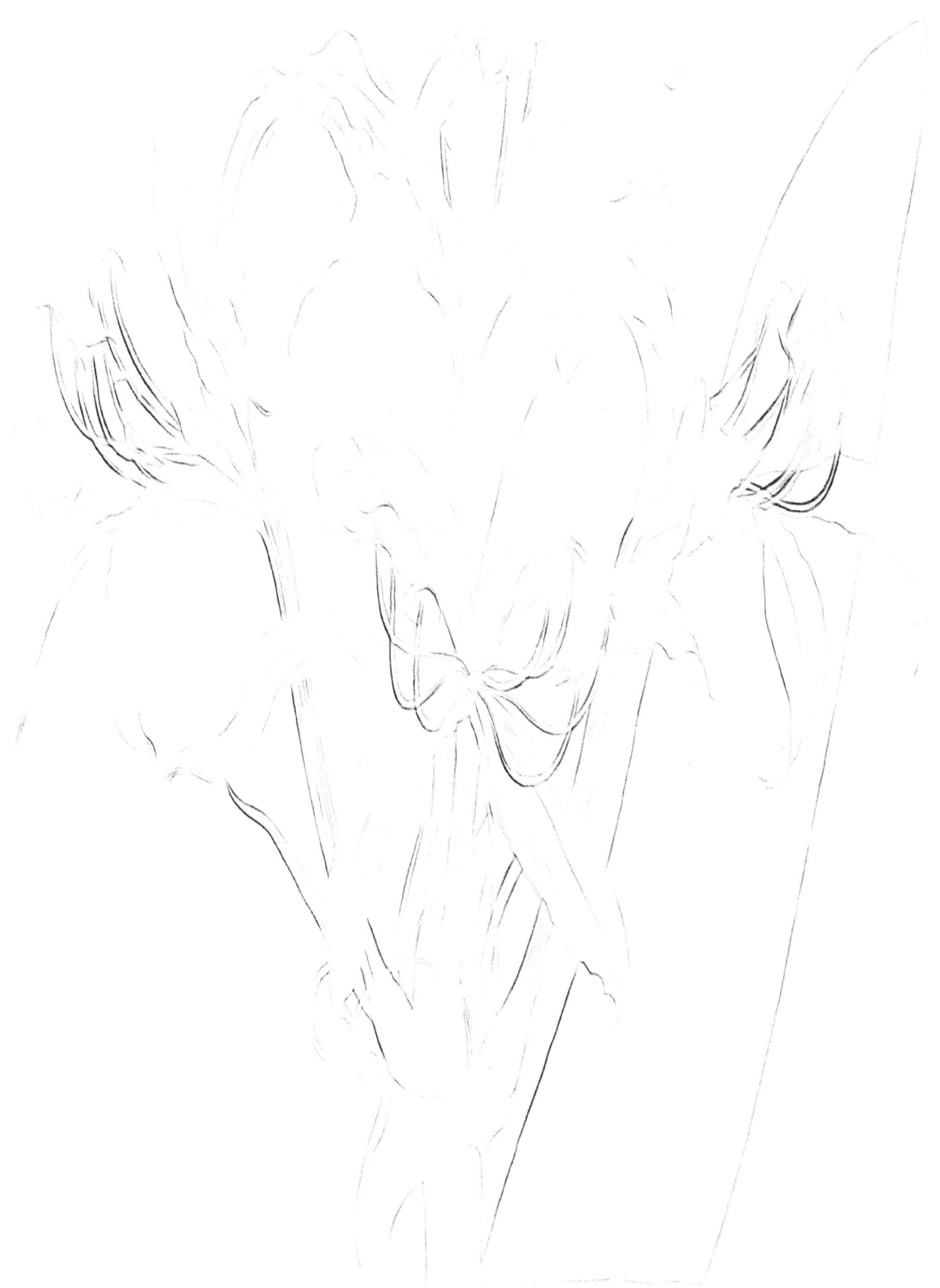

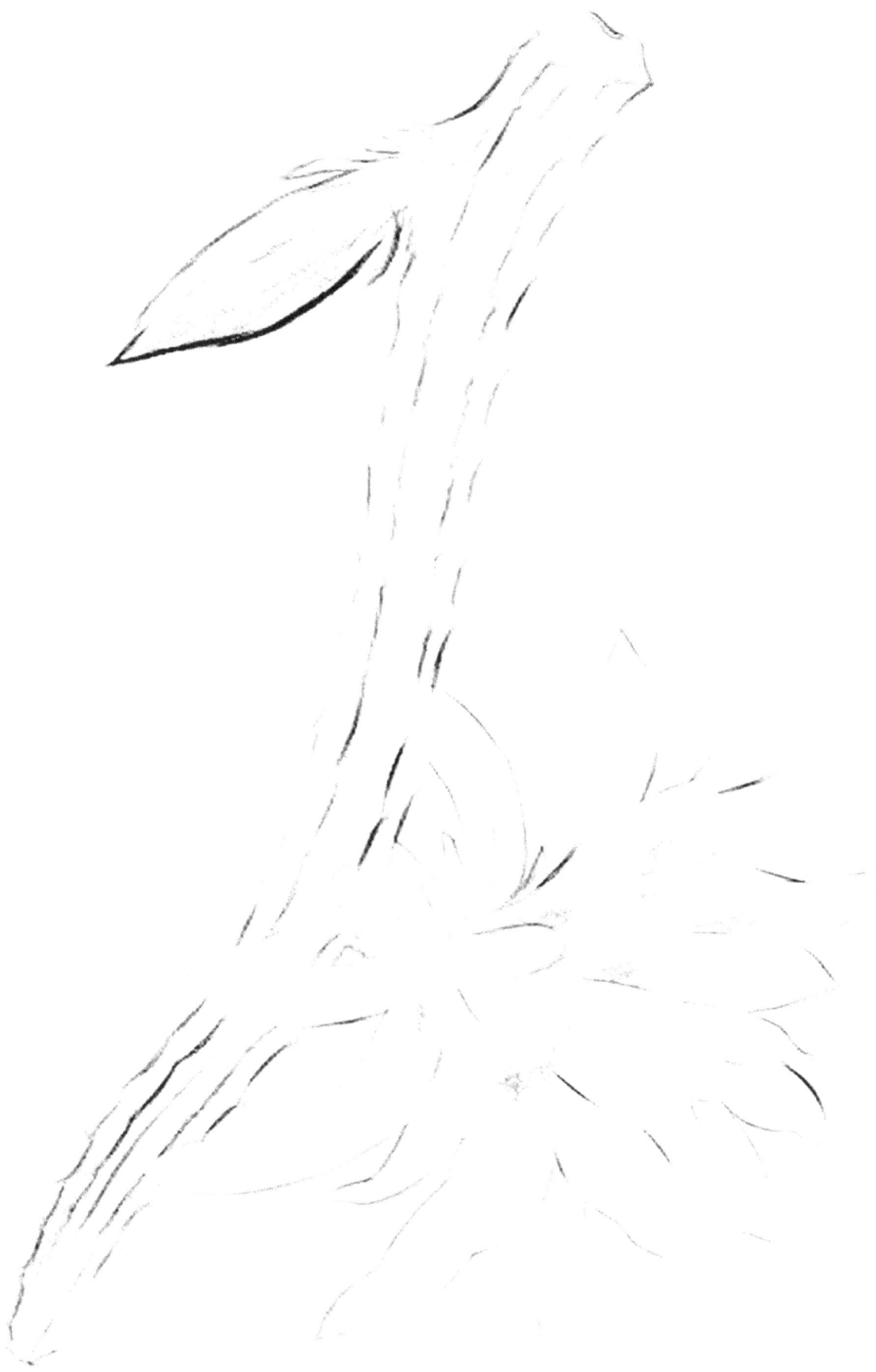

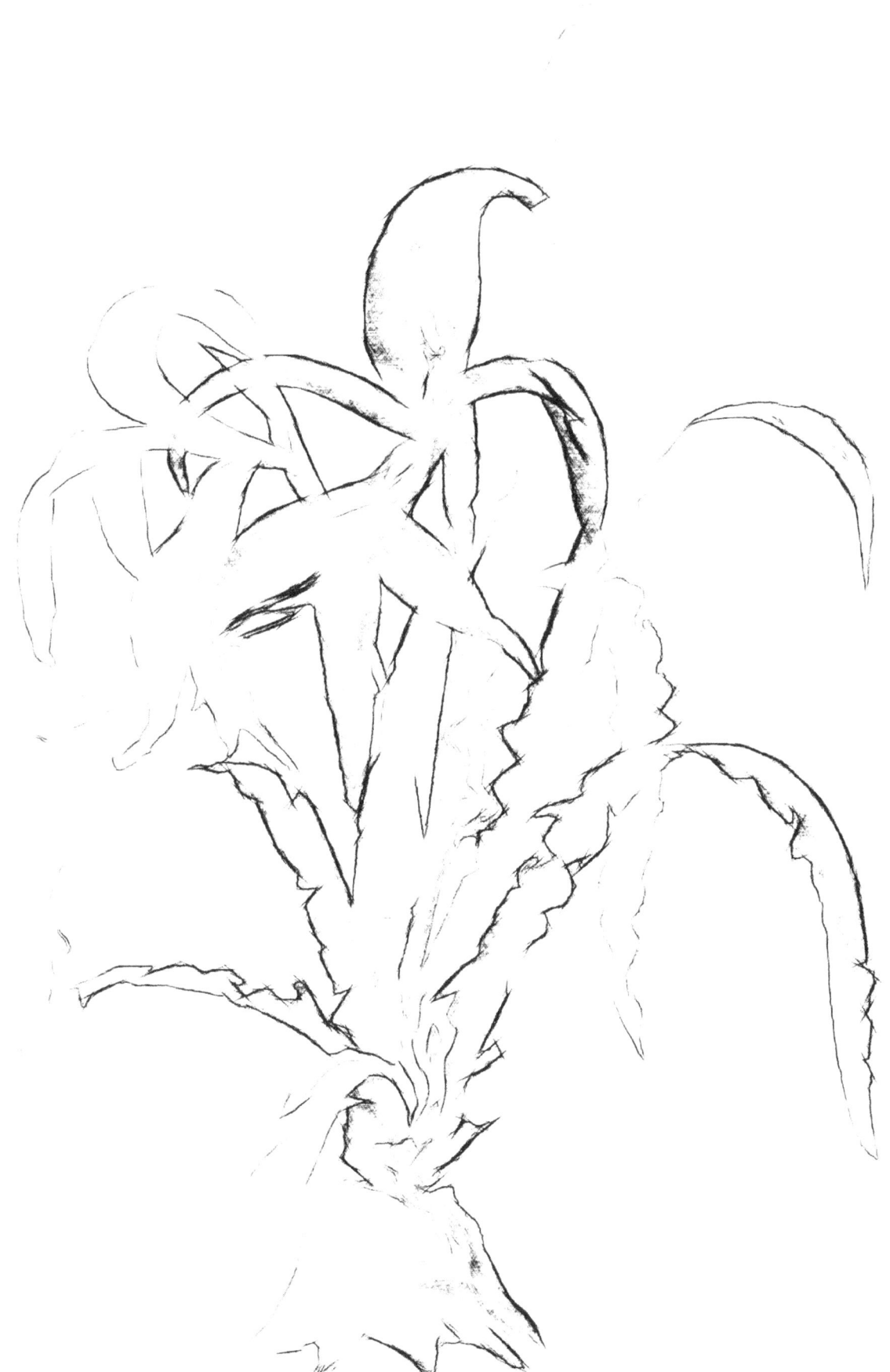

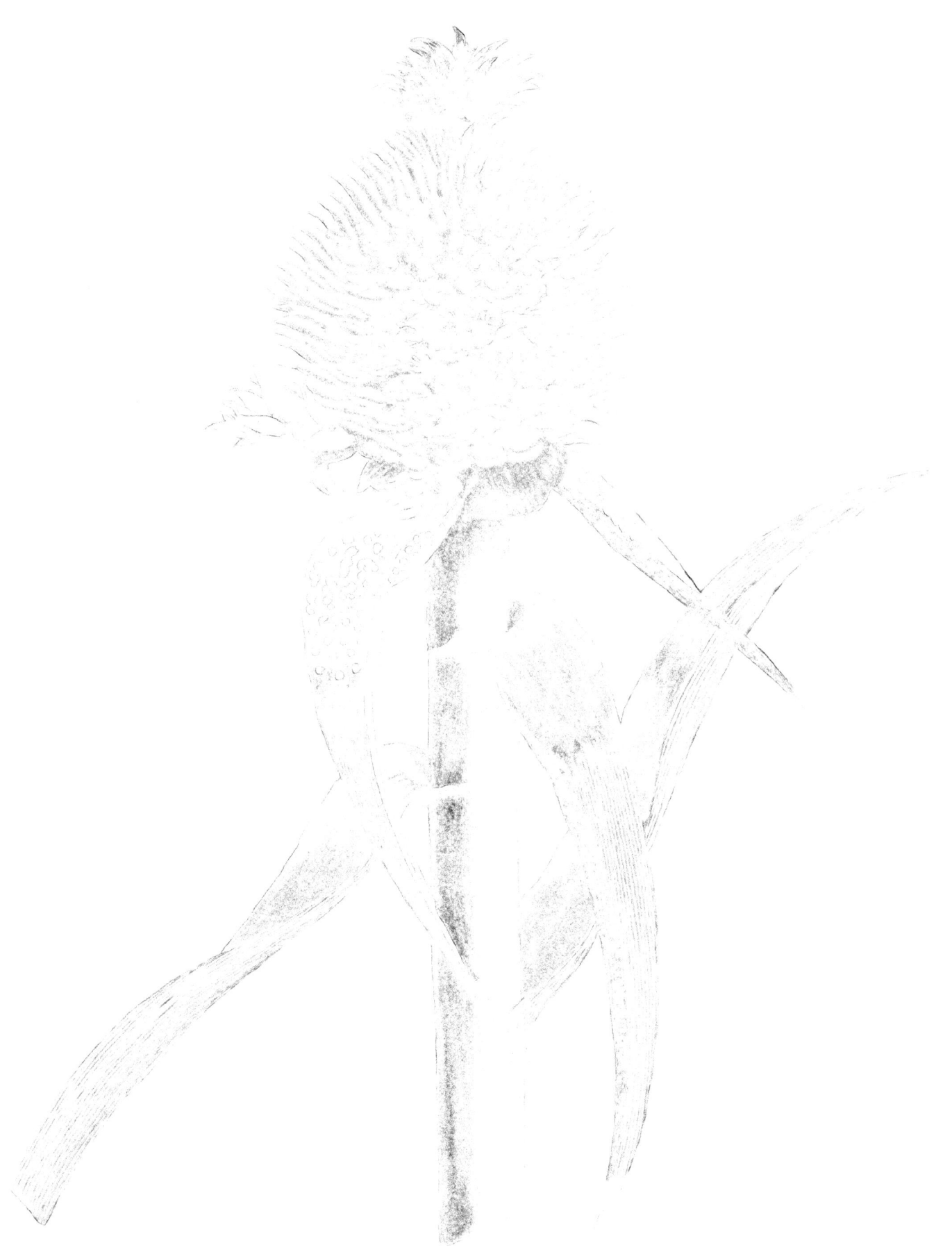

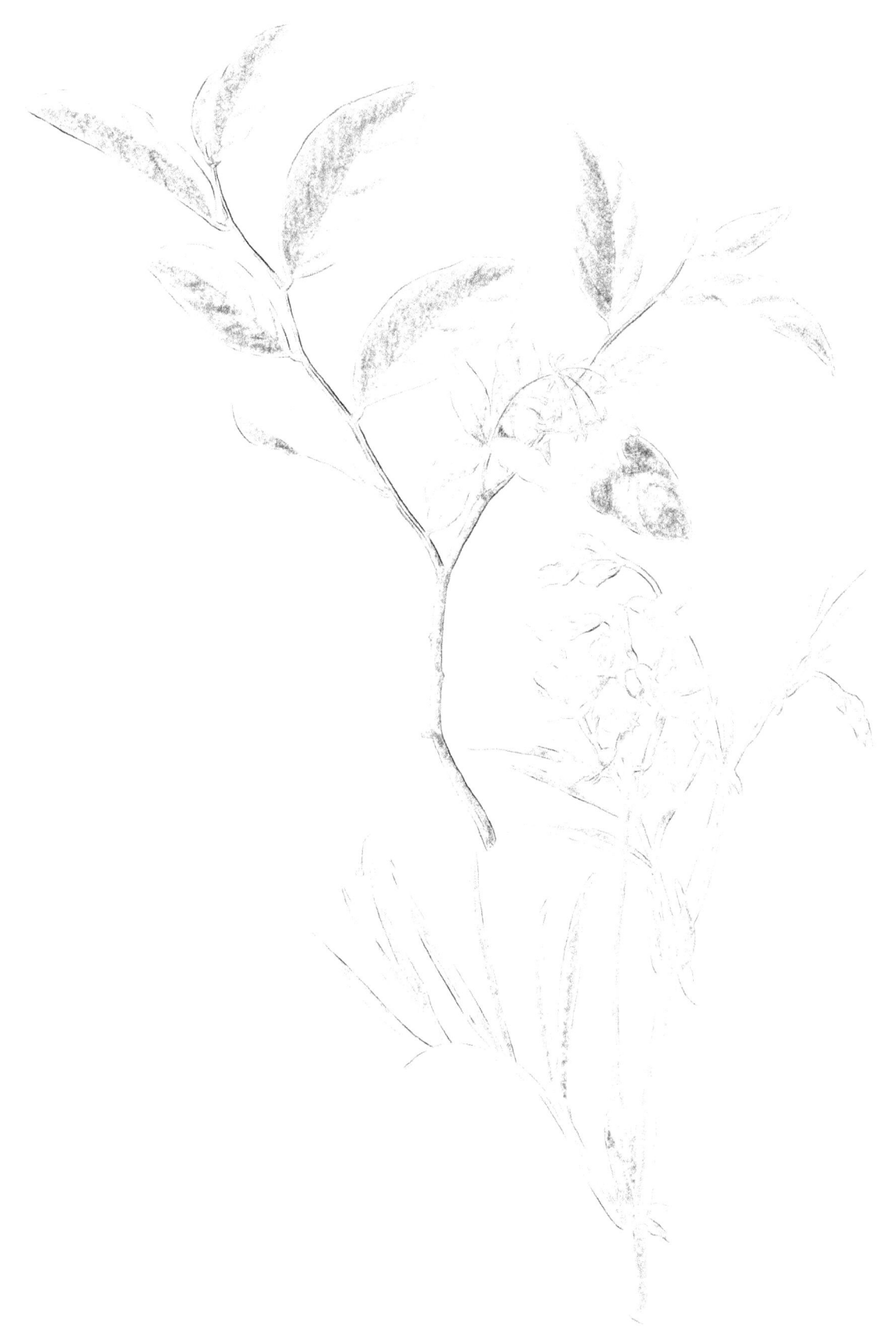

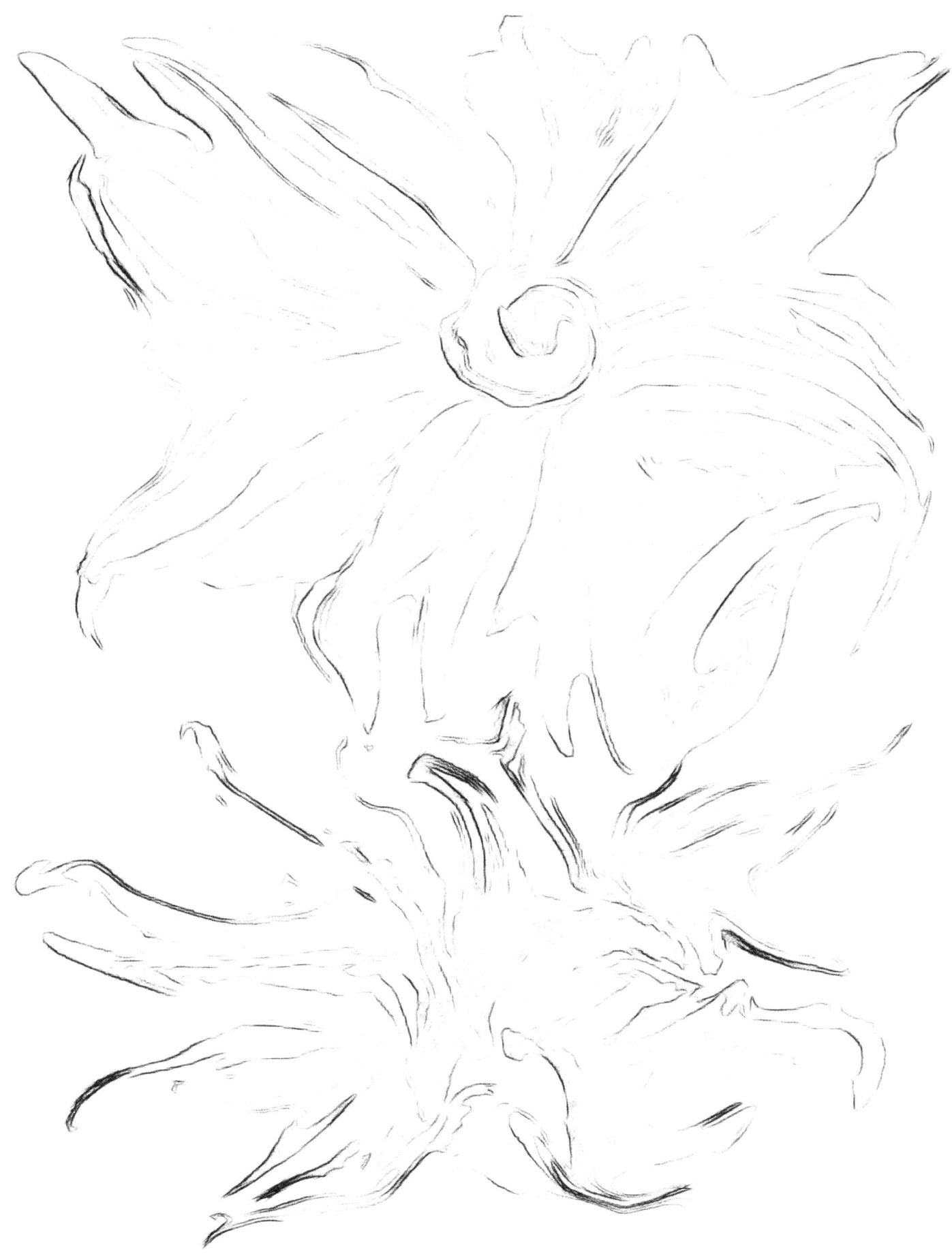

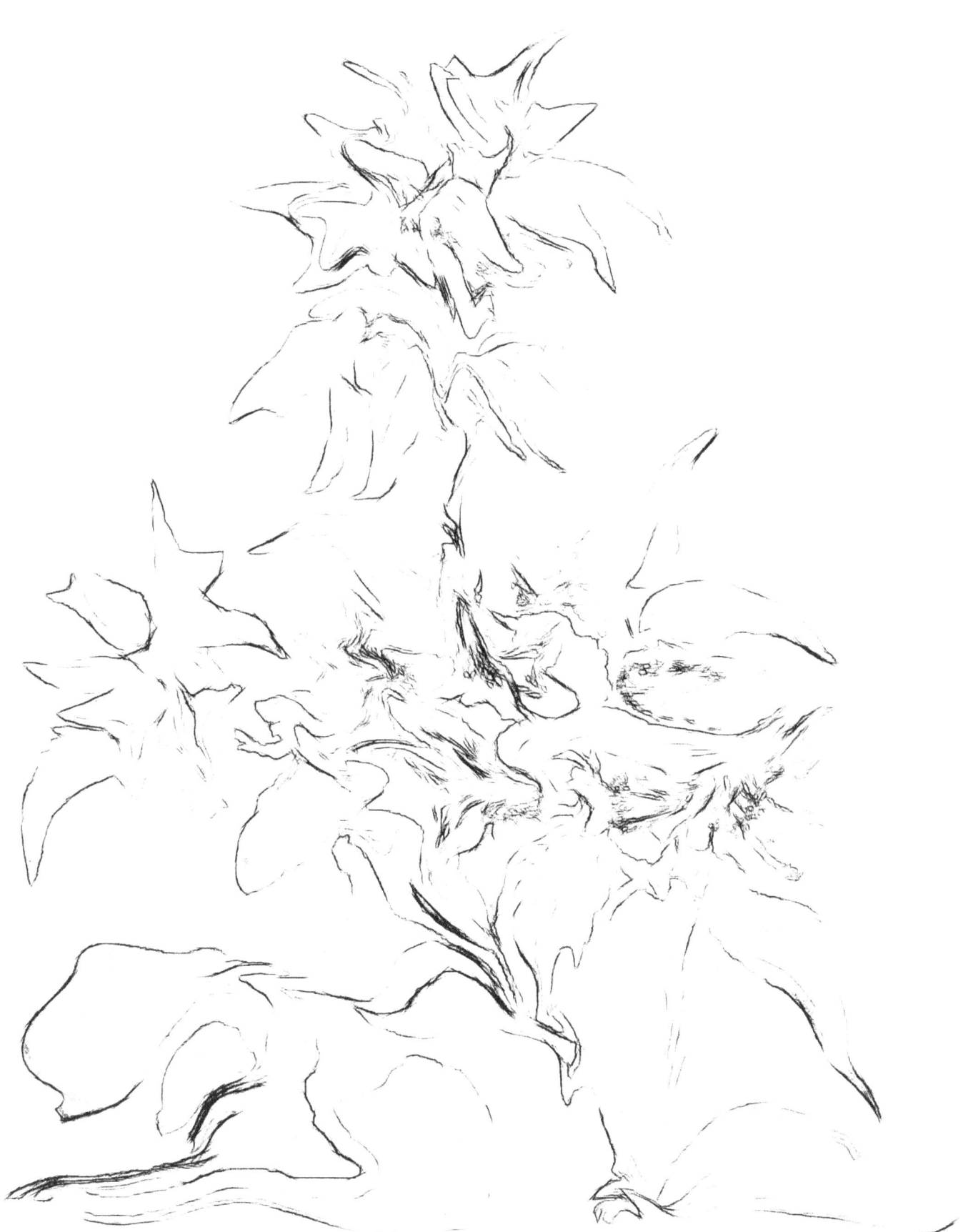

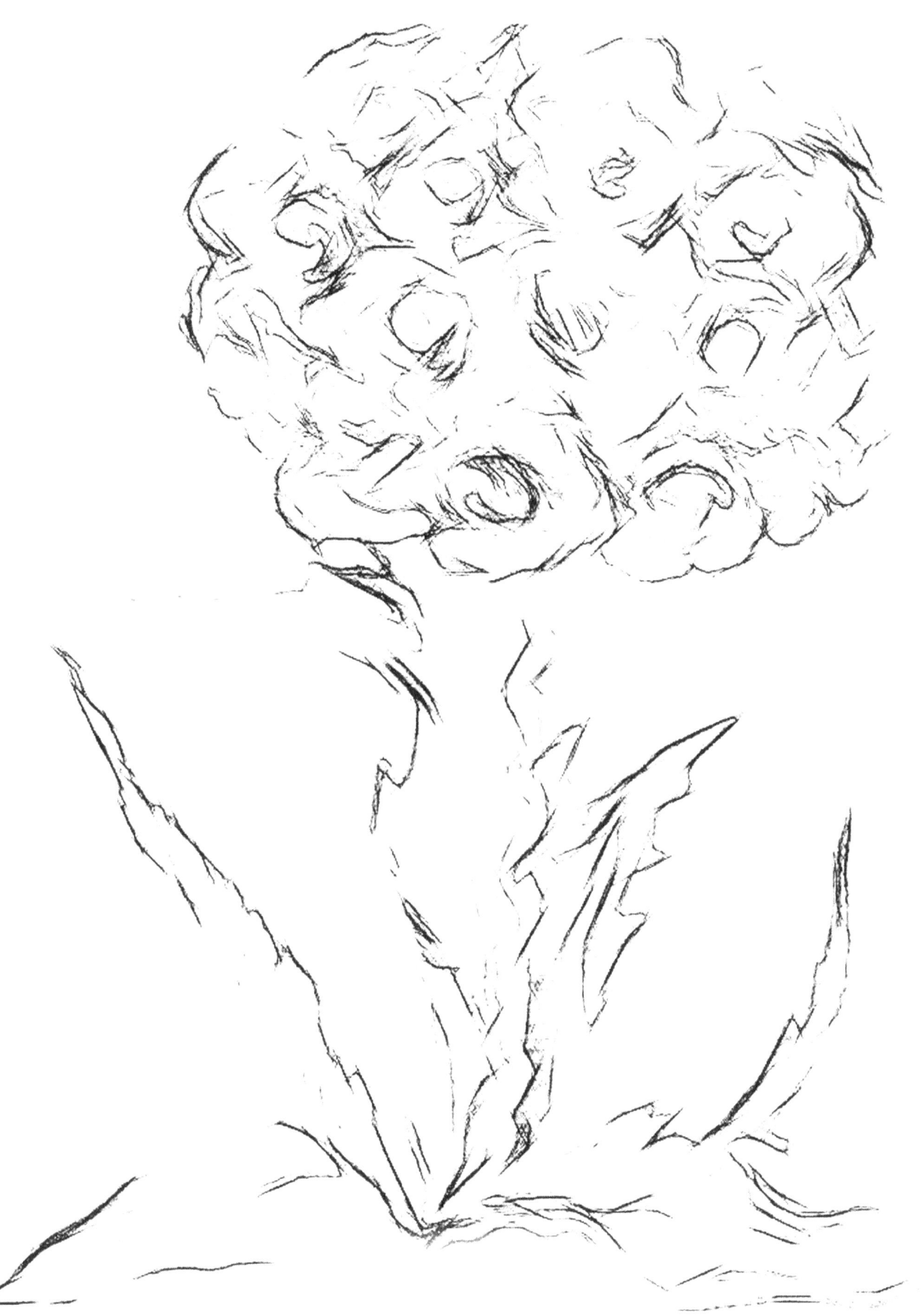

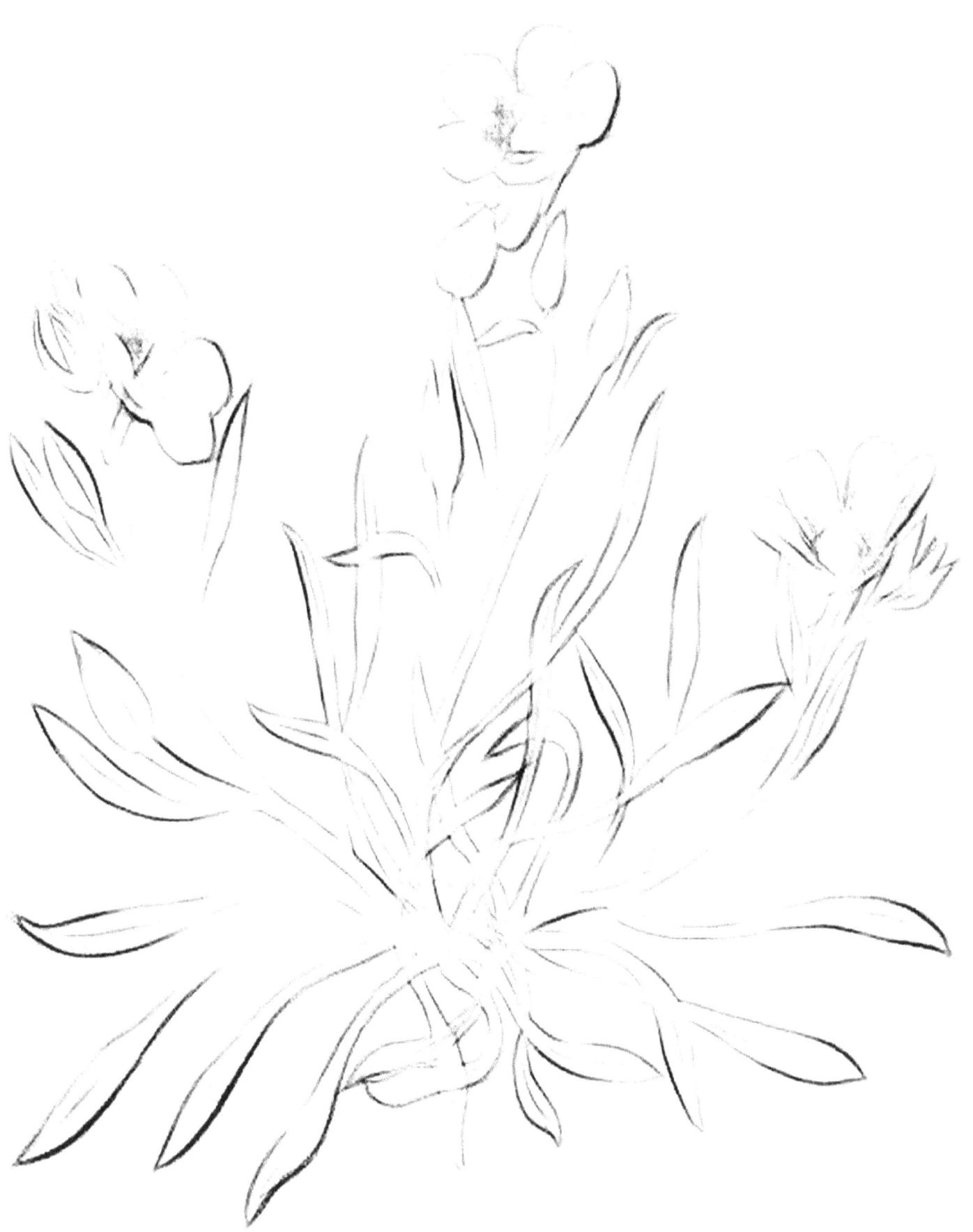

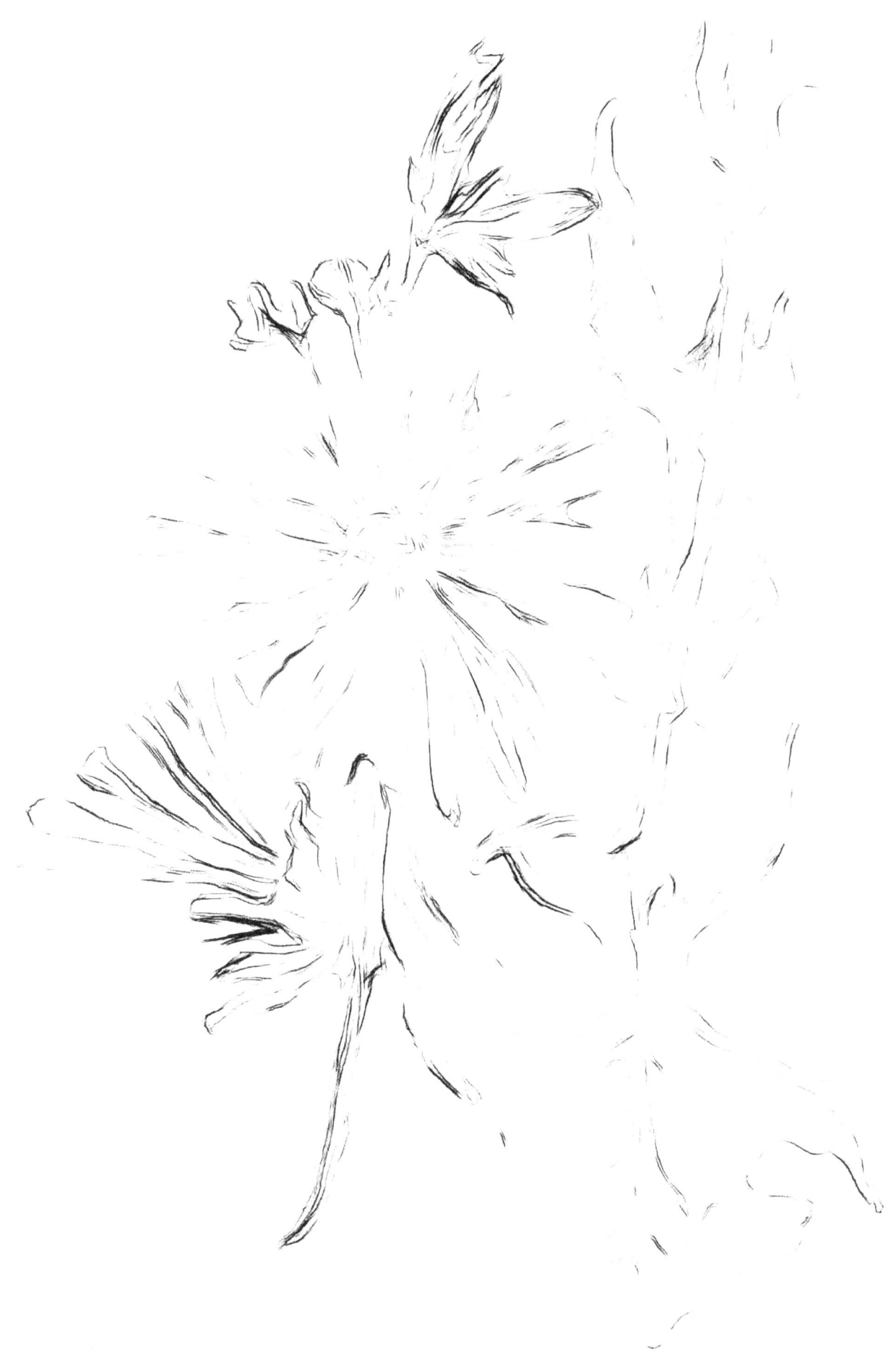

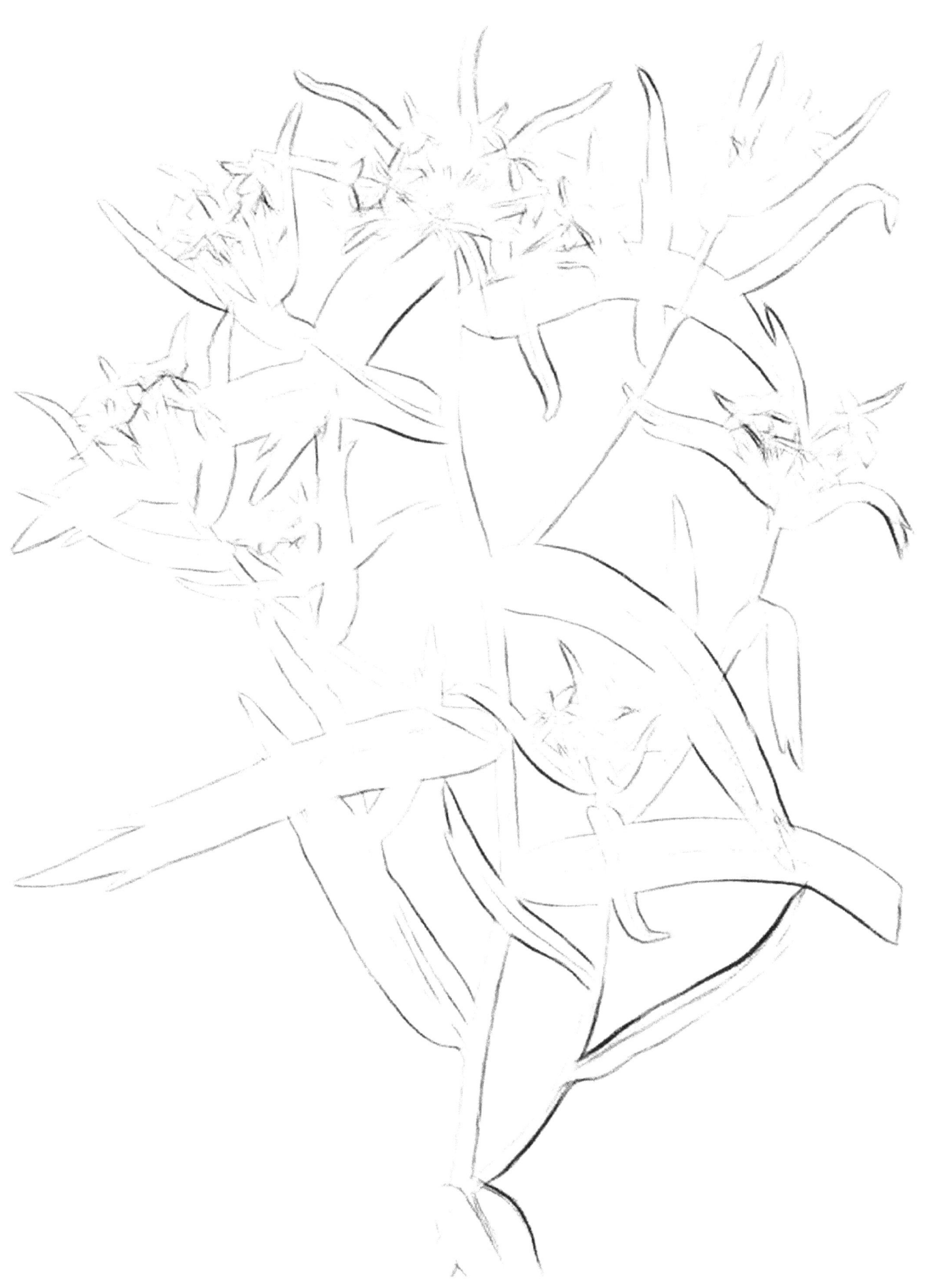

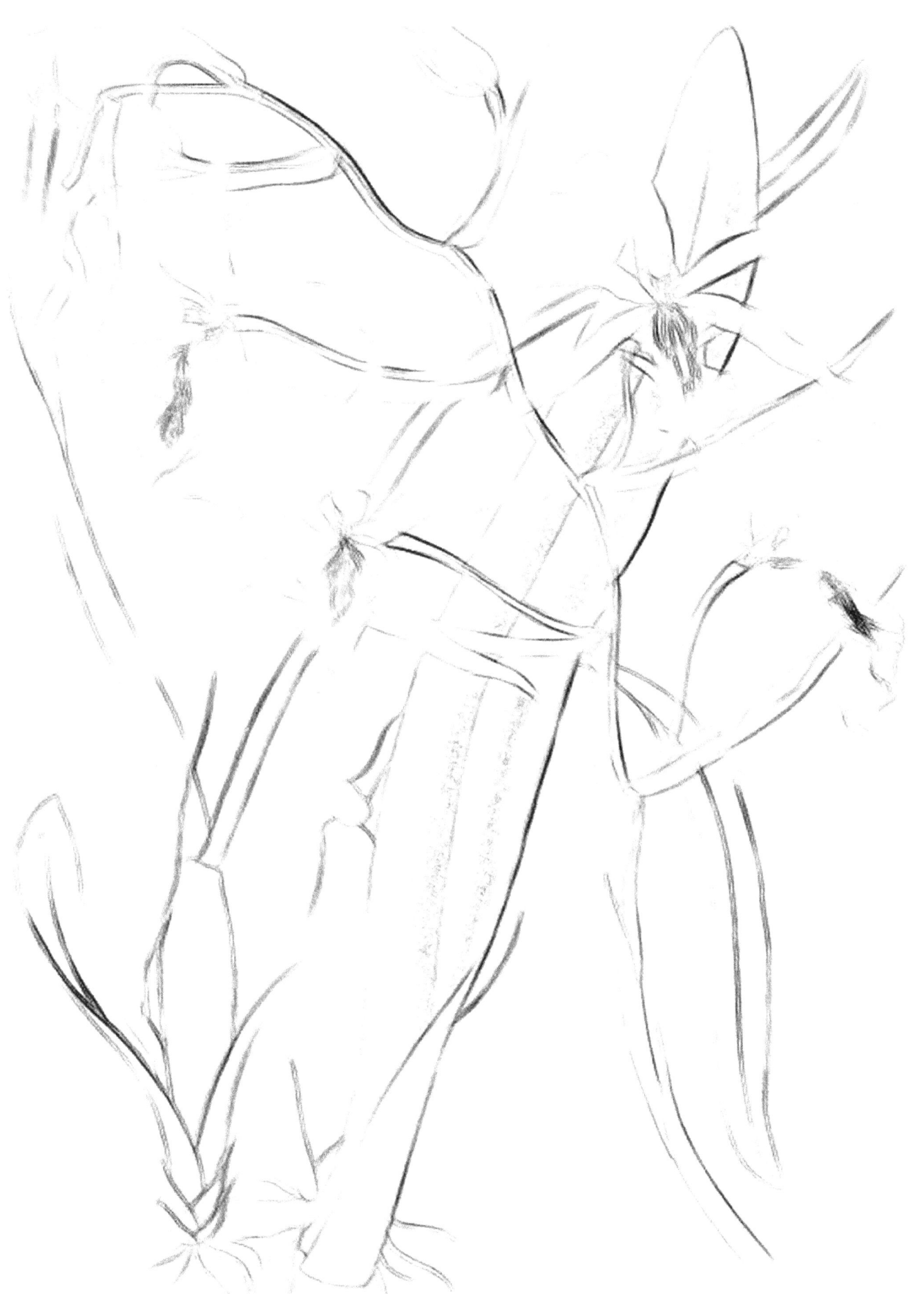

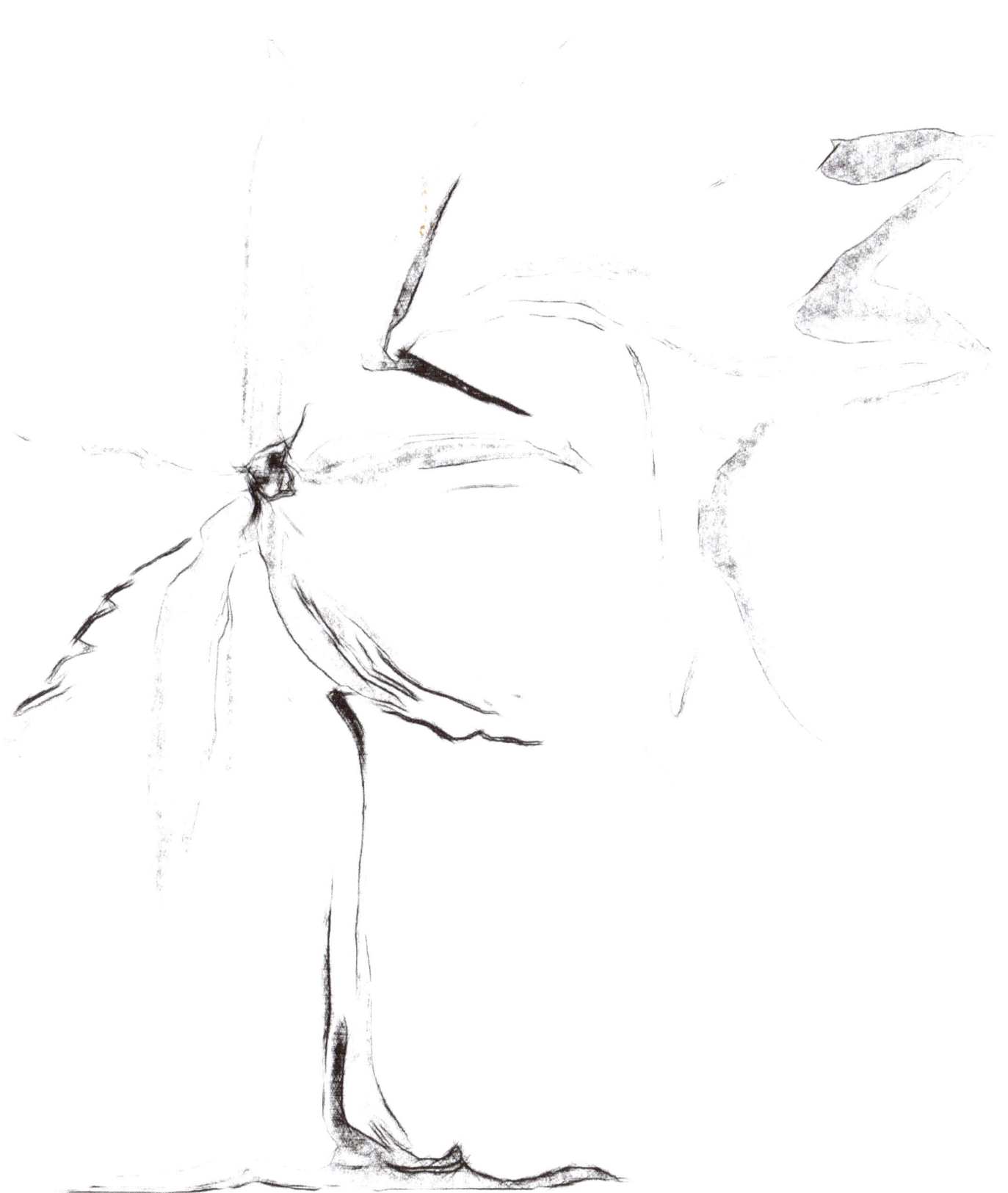

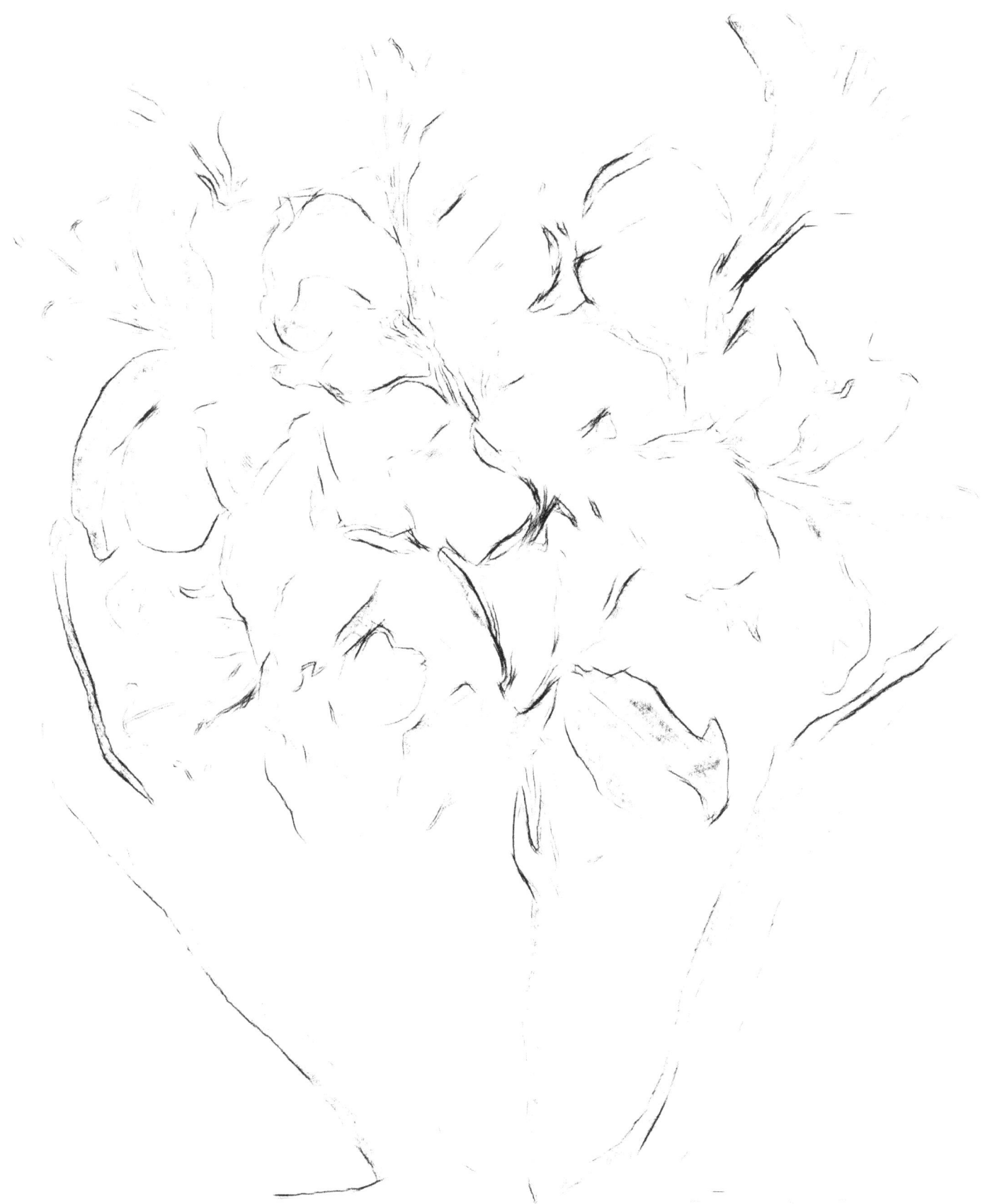

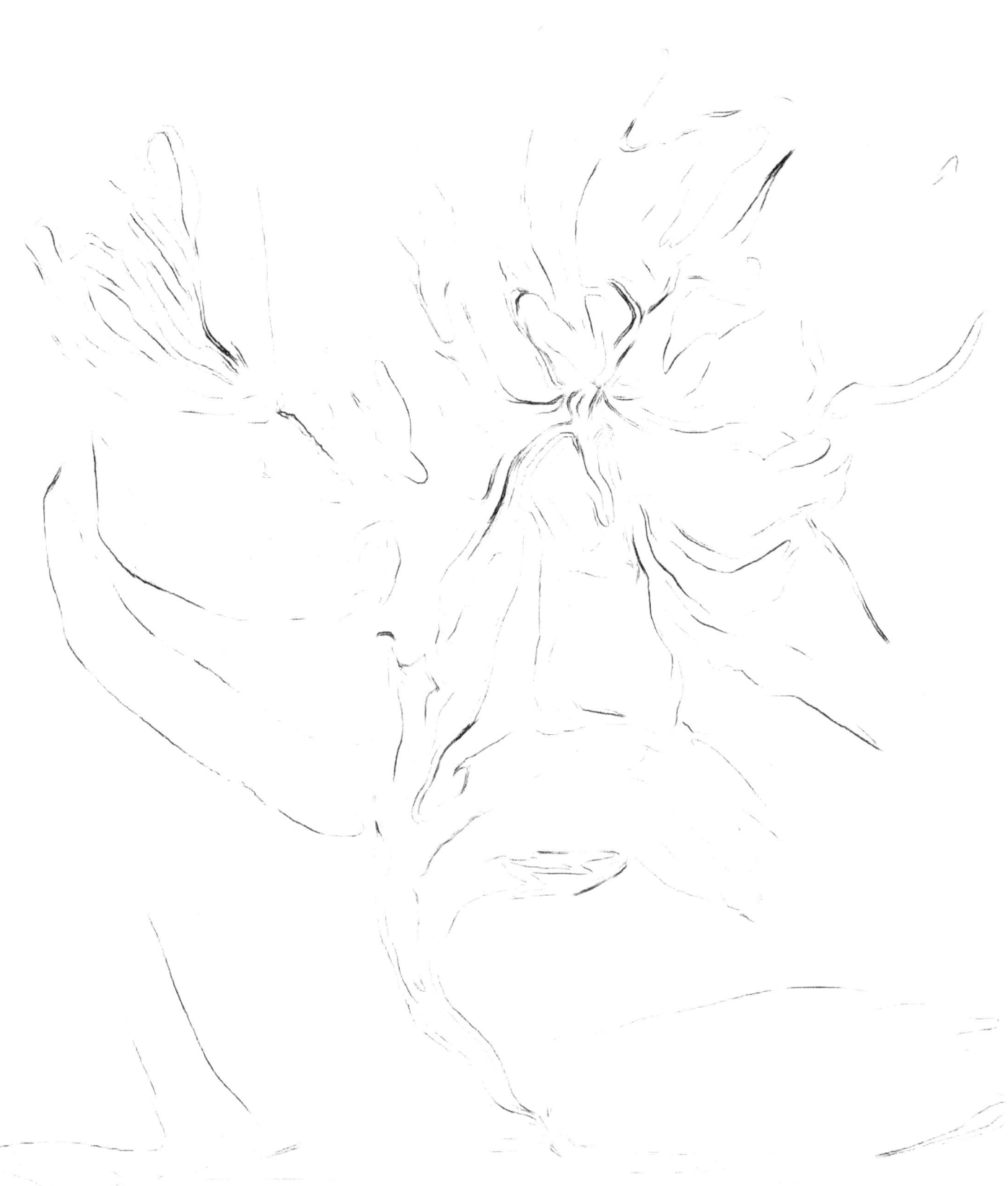

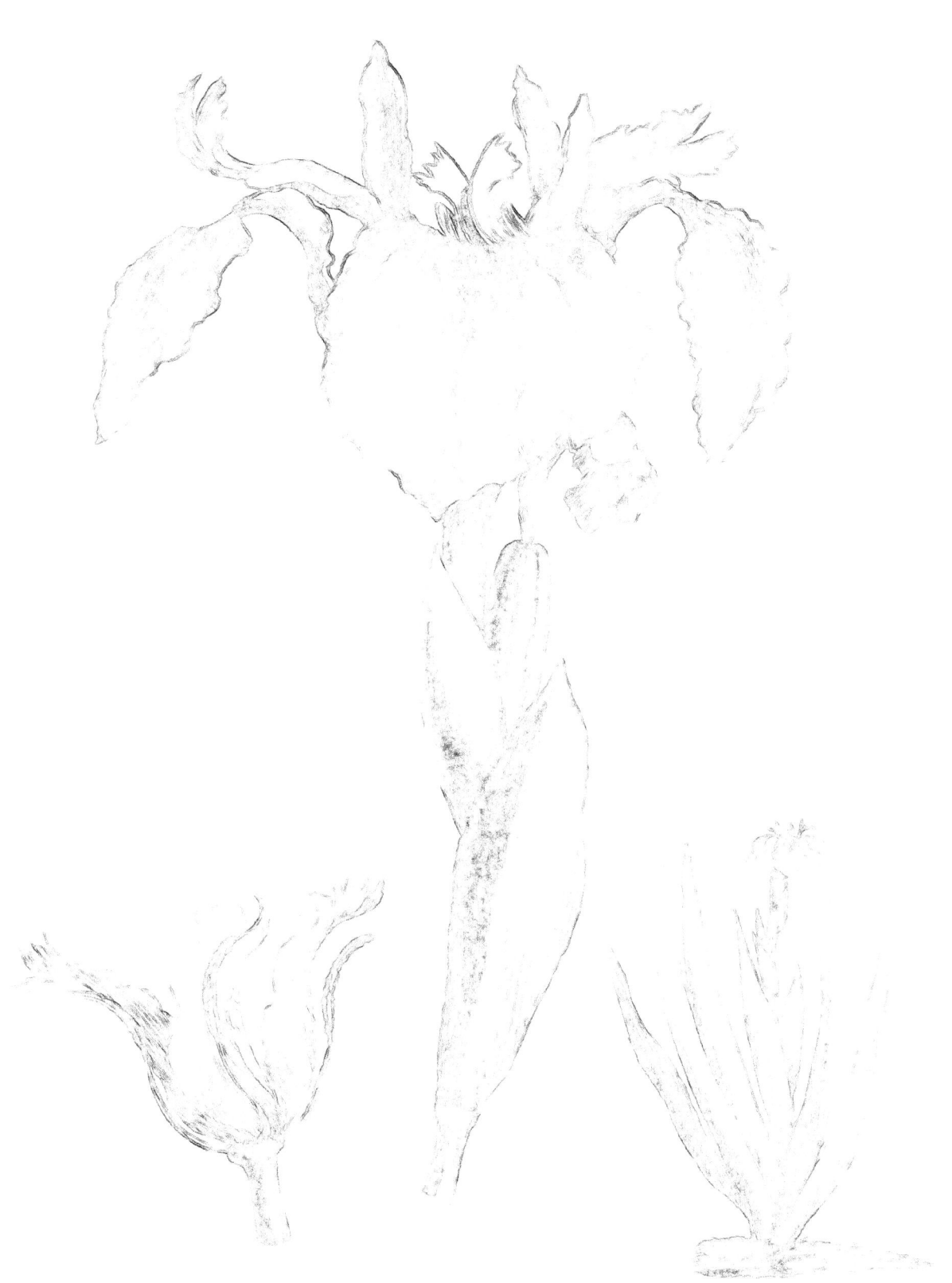

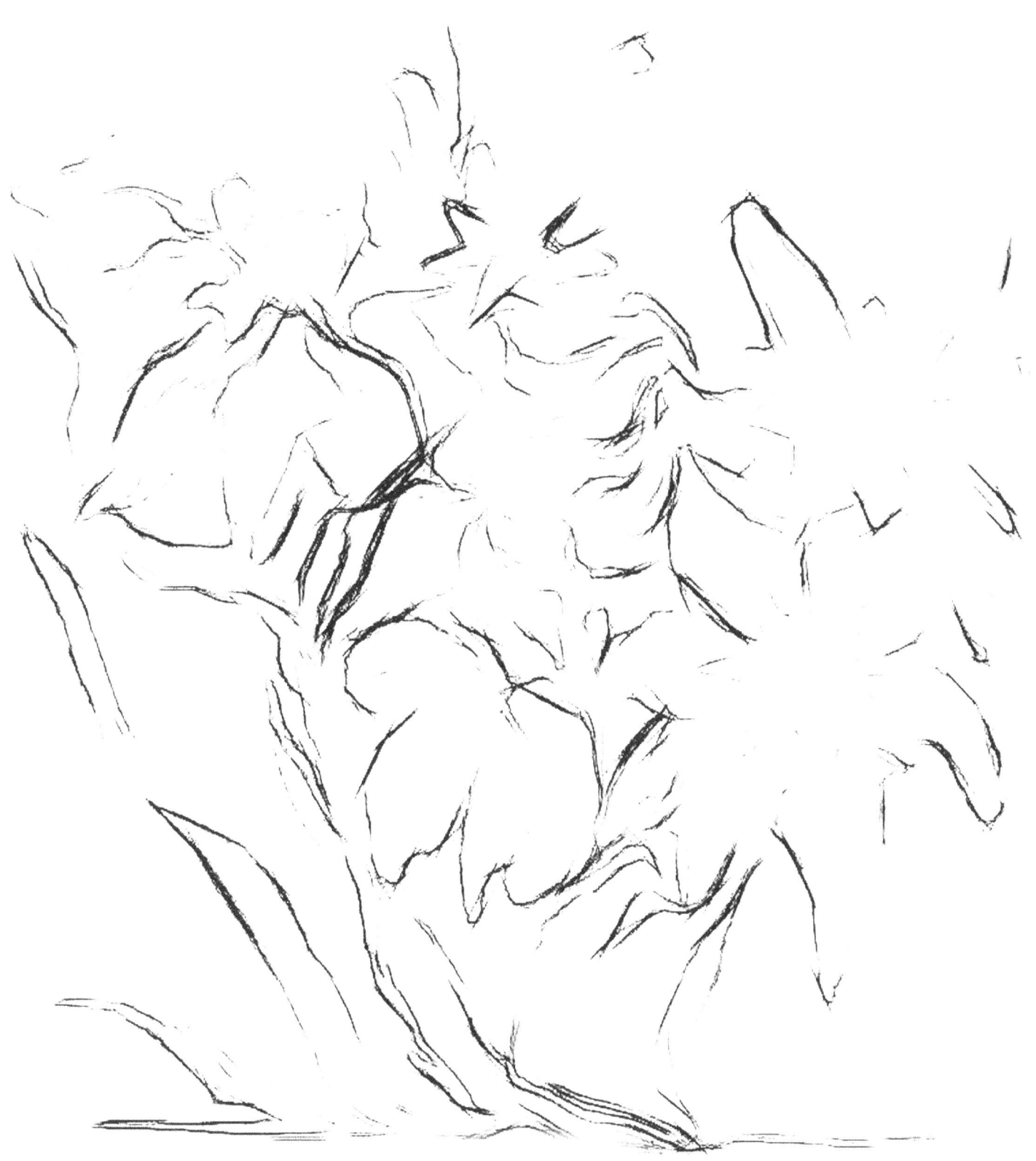

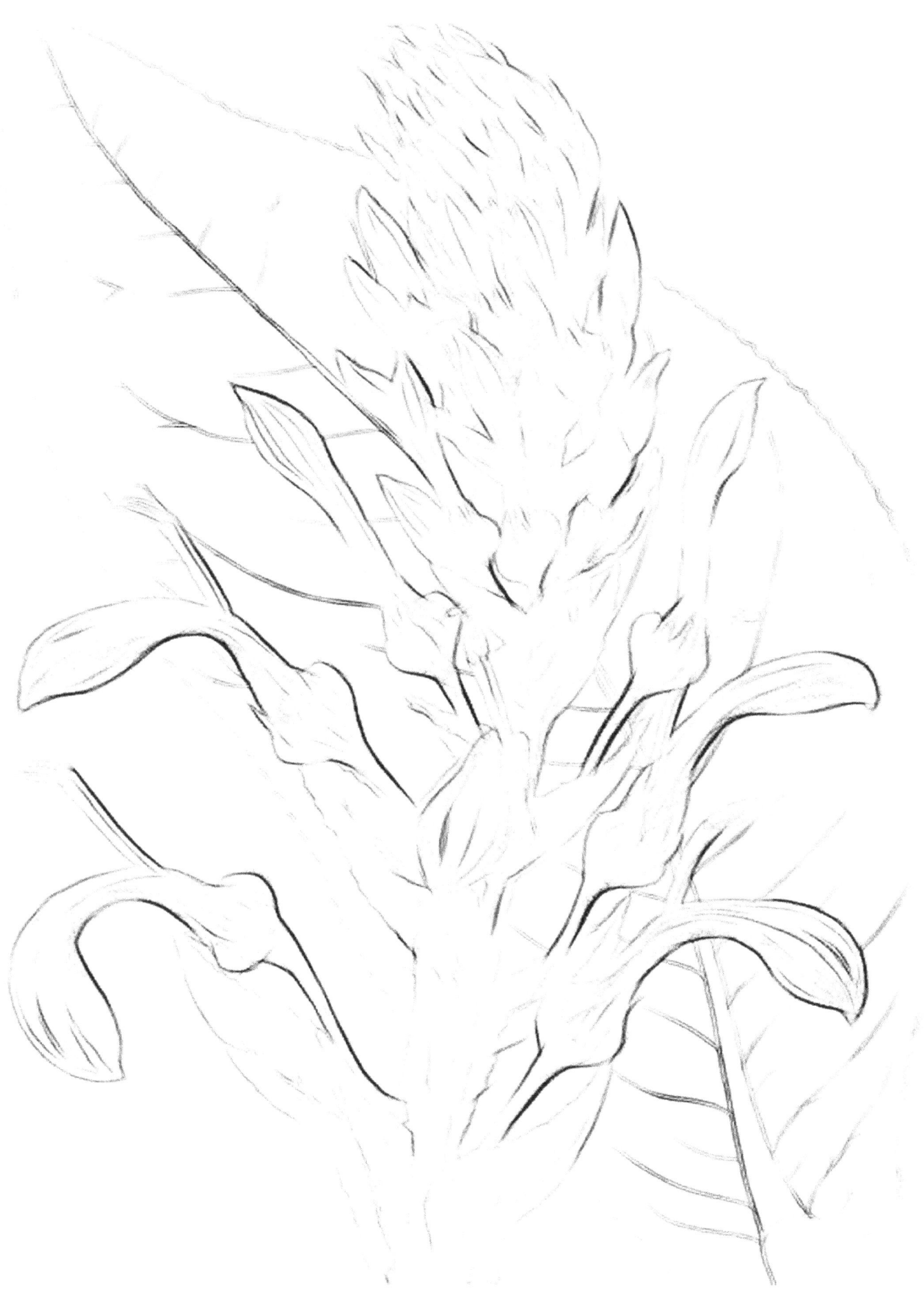

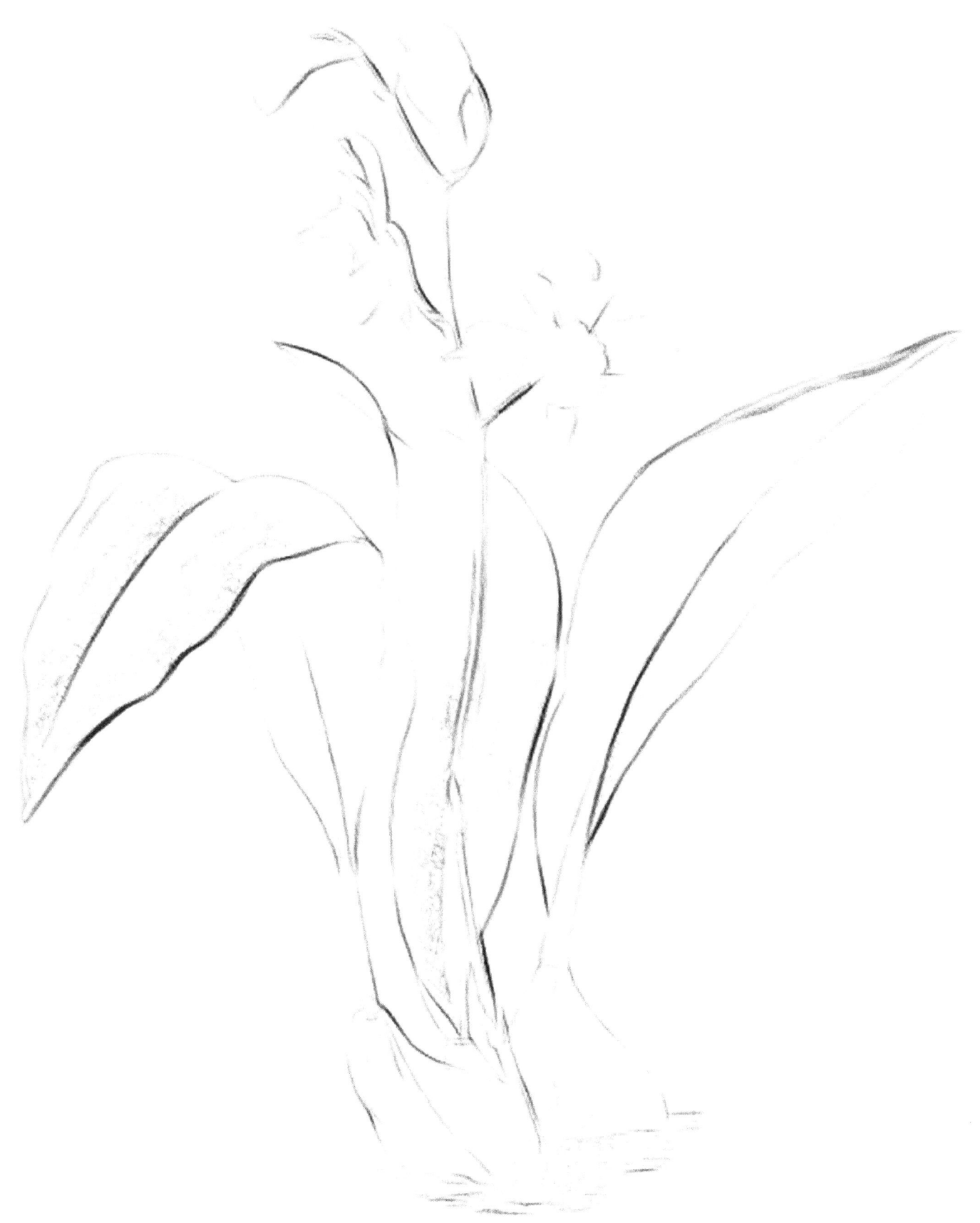

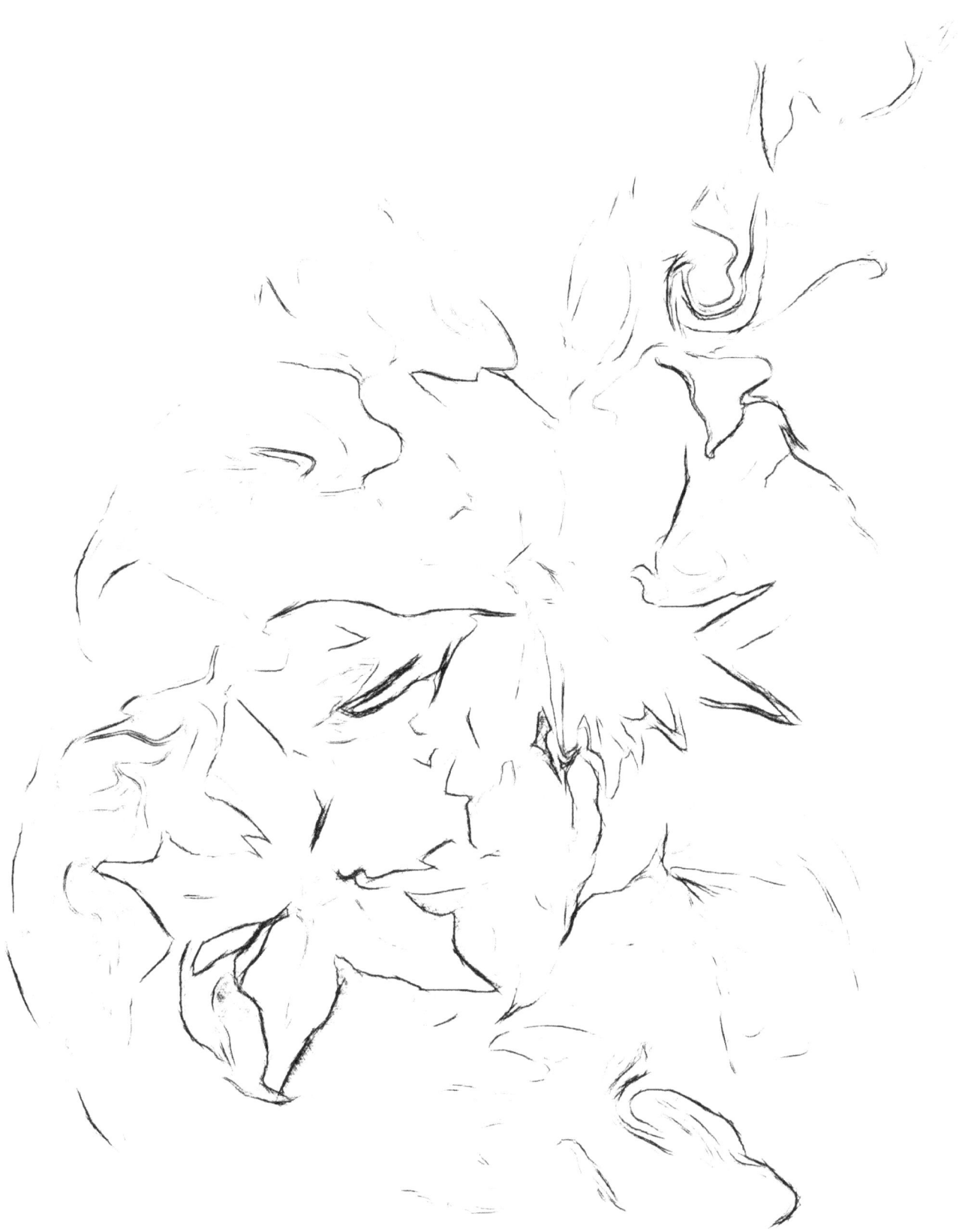

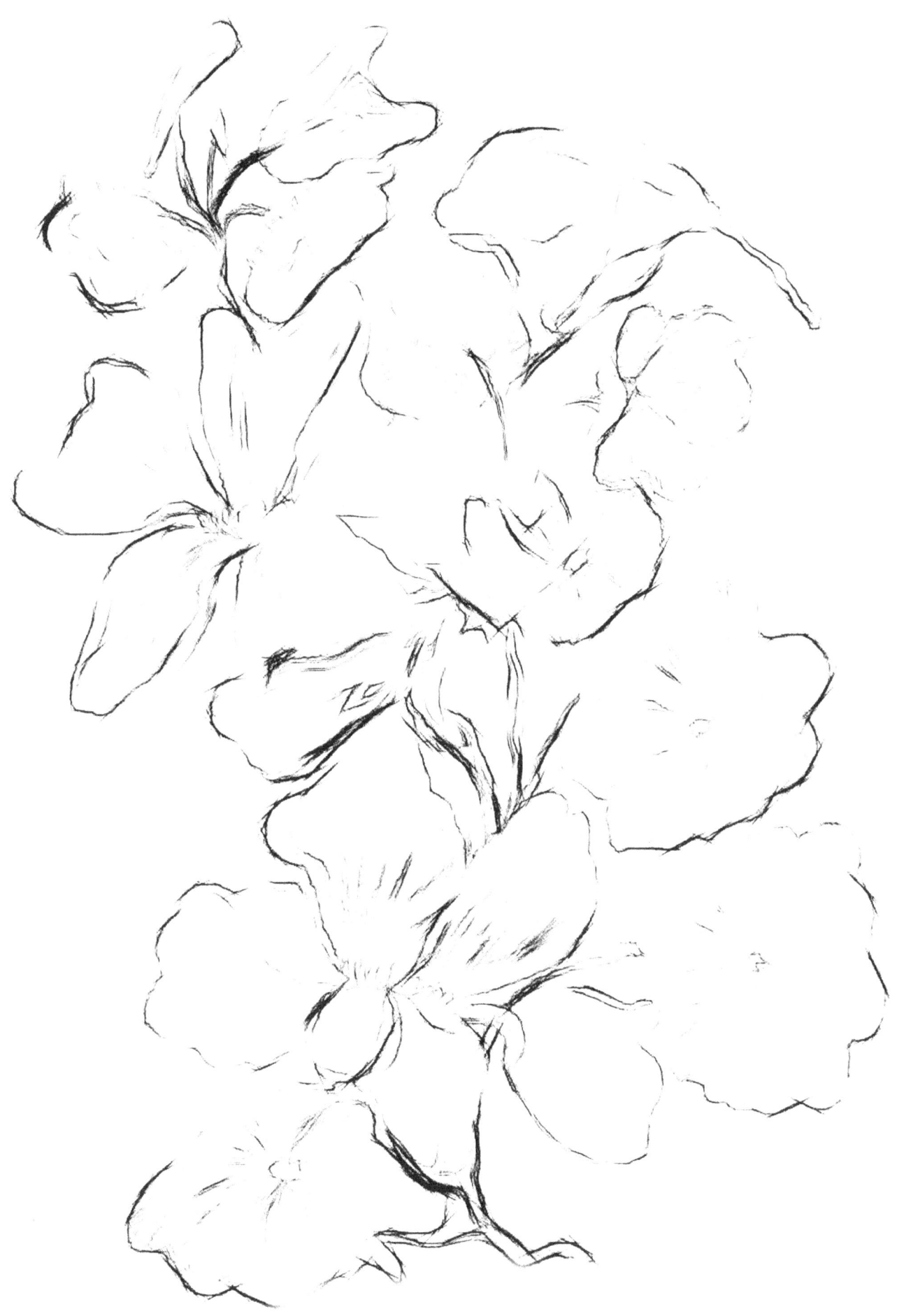

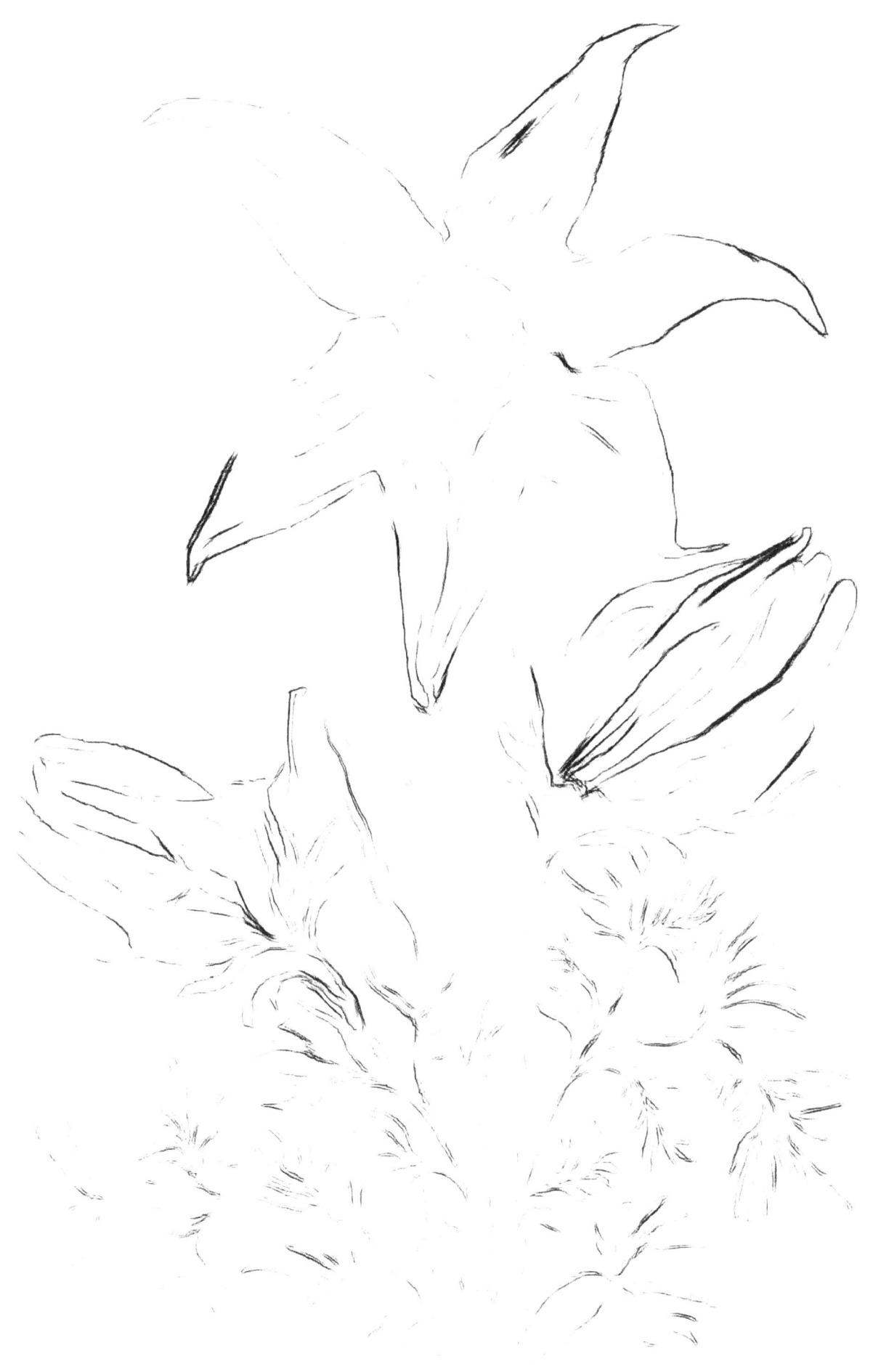

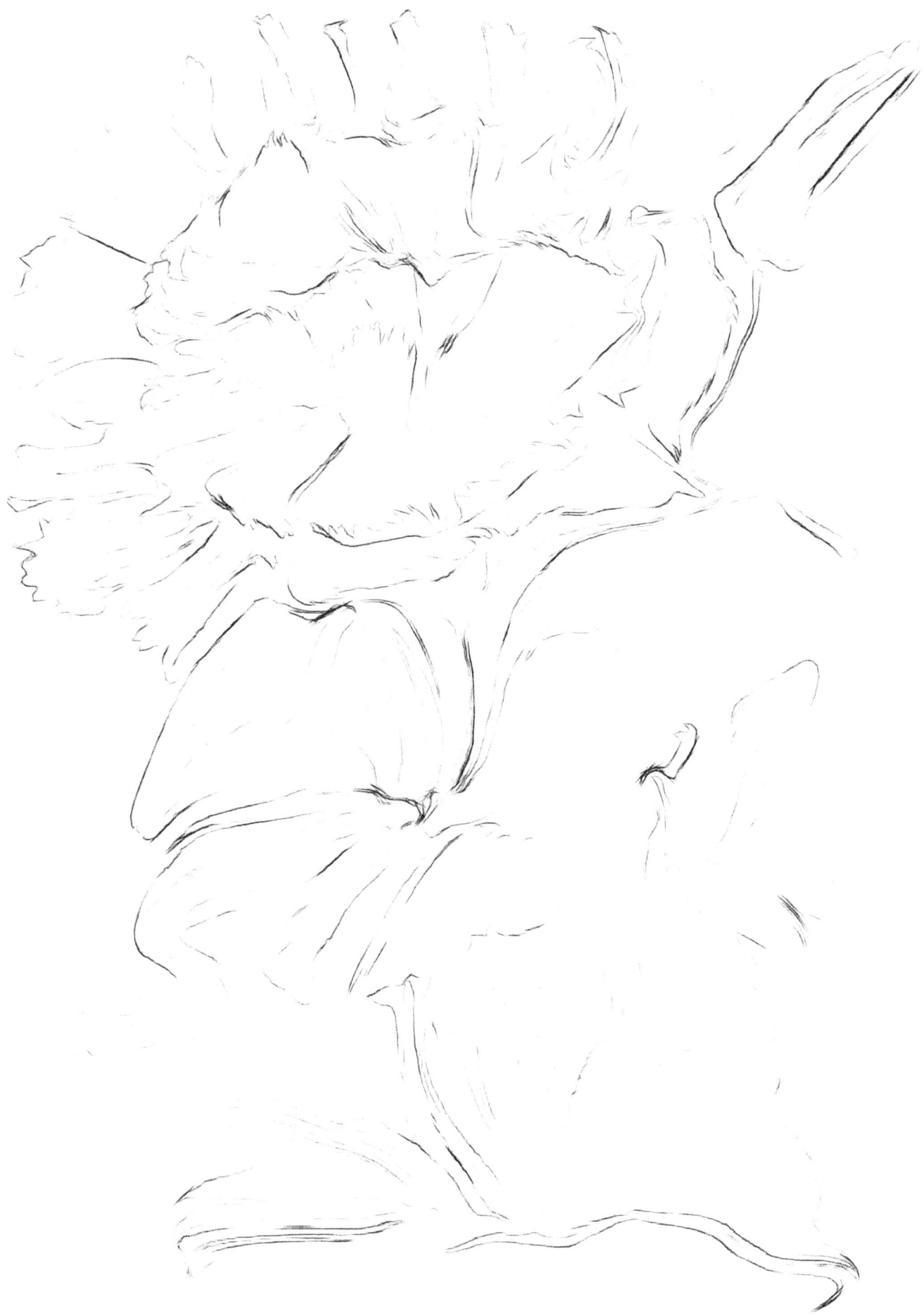